PENGUIN FOLKLORE LIBRARY

THE CINDERELLA STORY

Advisory Editor: Neil Philip

Neil Philip was born in York in 1955. He now lives in Buckinghamshire, where he divides his time between writing and research and his work as editorial director of a small publishing company. His consuming interest is folk narrative, but he has also written on children's literature and on English social history. His essays and reviews have appeared in numerous journals, including *The Times*, *The Times Educational Supplement*, *The Times Literary Supplement* and *Folklore*, of which he is a former reviews editor. Among his other books are *A Fine Anger: A Critical Introduction to the Work of Alan Garner* (1981), winner of the ChLA Literary Criticism Book Award; a country anthology, *Between Earth and Sky* (Penguin 1984); and *The Tale of Sir Gawain* (1987), shortlisted for the Emil/Kurt Maschler Award. He has contributed two other titles in the Penguin Folklore Library, of which he is also advisory editor, *English Folktales* and *Scottish Folktales*. With Victor Neuburg he has edited a selection of Charles Dickens's social journalism, *A December Vision* (1986).

THE CINDERELLA STORY

NEIL PHILIP

PENGUIN BOOKS

PENGUIN BOOKS
Published by the Penguin Group
27 Wrights Lane, London W8 5TZ, England
Viking Penguin Inc., 40 West 23rd Street, New York, New York 10010, USA
Penguin Books Australia Ltd, Ringwood, Victoria, Australia
Penguin Books Canada Ltd, 2801 John Street, Markham, Ontario, Canada L3R 1B4
Penguin Books (NZ) Ltd, 182–190 Wairau Road, Auckland 10, New Zealand

Penguin Books Ltd, Registered Offices: Harmondsworth, Middlesex, England

First published 1989
1 3 5 7 9 10 8 6 4 2

Made and printed in Great Britain by
Richard Clay Ltd, Bungay, Suffolk
Typeset in 11/13pt Lasercomp Garamond by
C. R. Barber & Partners (Highlands) Ltd, Fort William

For Emma

Contents

Contents

Preface

Of all the world's folktales, 'Cinderella' is perhaps the most familiar. Perrault's classic version has been made the basis of countless retellings. Everyone encounters the story in childhood, and recognizes it in adult life, whether in an opera or an advertisement. Yet this familiarity – as I hope this book will show – is partial and misleading. Cinderella's story is much stranger and much richer than the accepted version.

I have linked a number of complete Cinderella texts with a commentary that attempts to clarify their tangled history. In doing so, I depend very heavily on the work of others, and in particular on three books, each models of their type and date. Marian Roalfe Cox's *Cinderella*, commissioned by the Folklore Society and published by it in 1893, was the first thorough investigation on scientific lines of a single story and its variants. In it, she abstracted 345 (mostly European) narratives and listed their chief incidents. The publication of this ground-breaking work caused a little flurry of essays and speculation on the Cinderella story, which has also been valuable. Cox's work was extended though not superseded in 1951 by Anna Birgitta Rooth's *The Cinderella Cycle*. Rooth's study is organized on the principles of the Finnish 'historic-geographic' school, and offers a marvellously succinct and penetrating account of the history and geographical distribution of Cinderella tales. Rooth had access to over twice as many versions as Cox, notably from Eastern Europe, Indo-China and the Near East. In 1982 both these studies were complemented by Alan Dundes's *Cinderella: A Folklore Casebook*, an admirably arranged and annotated selection of critical comment on the Cinderella cycle. Dundes's book also contains a valuable bibliography.

All three of these books represent a scrupulous and exacting scholarship. But in dealing with such exceedingly complex material, all three scholars necessarily move beyond the realm of interest of the general reader who is not an expert in folktale study. This book claims no advance on their work. It is, instead, an attempt to convey the entertaining variety of the world's Cinderella stories through the stories themselves, rather than analysis of them.

Neil Philip
1988

Introduction

A folktale is not just the spoken equivalent of a literary short story. It has no set text, but is endlessly re-created in the telling. It is one of the aims of this book, by juxtaposing widely varying tales which are nevertheless formed from the same matrix, to offer readers a chance to explore this essential difference between the spoken and the written story. The texts gathered in it are not definitive. While they do work as short stories, offering humour, drama and tragedy within a structured plot, they should be regarded simply as evidence of particular narrations, shorn from their context, unnaturally frozen on paper, and inevitably distorted by the very act of recording.

Such evidence has been gathered, set down and interpreted in many different ways. It is very rare to see, even in academic publications, strict verbatim transcripts of oral narratives. The words in the air are not the same words on the page. For the reader, the flow of words, intonation, gesture, cadence, must be turned into sentence and paragraph, fixed on the flat white page. At its best, as in Linda Williamson's alert, sensitive transcription of her husband Duncan Williamson's Scottish traveller version of Cinderella (see pp. 161–73), some of the intimacy of the original telling shines through. At worst, you are left with a simple summary of what happened next, a bare record of words spoken or, in earlier days, a refurbished literary interpretation of the original oral tale.

That is what we have in Perrault, whose astute shaping of French popular tales for a new courtly audience has so dominated our conception of Cinderella.

In many ways, as this book will show, Perrault's 'Cendrillon' is an untypical Cinderella story, in its knowing tone, in its concern for passing social detail, and in its whimsical embellishments – the rat coachman, the pumpkin coach. But our literary culture has valued the written word so much more than the spoken one that Perrault's version, rather than being one among many, has come to seem the archetype, the 'correct' story.

The Cinderellas in modern children's picture and story books are almost always based, at some remove, on Perrault, with a consistent prettification of language and incident that takes them further and further from the robust vitality of the oral tale. Earlier, cheap chapbooks containing fairy tales based on Perrault's stories had a rapid and profound effect on, for instance, the stories told and enjoyed among the English poor. Remembering the storytelling of his childhood in his *Shepherd's Calendar*, John Clare recalls among local and cautionary tales, and such indigenous stories as 'Jack and the Beanstalk' and 'The Three Heads in the Well',

> *The tale of Cinderella told*
> *The winter thro and never old*
> *The faireys favourite and friend*
> *Who made her happy in the end*
> *The pumpkin that at her approach*
> *Was turned into a golden coach*
> *The rats that faireys magic knew*
> *And instantly to horses grew*
> *And coachmen ready at her call*
> *To drive her to the princes ball*
> *With fur changd jackets silver lind*
> *And tails hung neath their hats behind*
> *Where soon as met the princes sight*
> *She made his heart ach all the night*
> *The golden glove wi fingers small*
> *She lost while dancing in the hall*
> *That was on every finger tryd*
> *And fitted hers and none beside*
> *When cinderella soon as seen*
> *Was woo'd and won and made a queen.*

Despite the replacement of the glass slipper with a golden glove, this is clearly a recollection of a version derived from Perrault.

This book is an attempt to explore behind Perrault's glittering façade: to recover the sense of surprise and the sense of danger in a tale with which we may feel wearily familiar. For folktales are important: they encode, in what the nineteenth-century folklorist Joseph Jacobs called 'bright trains of images', a way of understanding and confronting our profoundest desires and fears. They are wise with the canny ambiguous wisdom of the Delphic oracle which, according to Heraclitus, 'neither declares nor conceals, but gives a sign'.

The stories that make up what has been called the Cinderella cycle, like many of the most frequently told and recorded folktales, explore from various angles the knot or cluster of tensions inherent in the nuclear family. There are numerous ways of categorizing the Cinderella variants, depending on the nature and the order of the incidents. Many areas have distinctive traditions. But it is essentially true to say that there are two main strands of story: one in which the girl is mistreated and humiliated because of her stepmother's jealousy, and one in which her suffering is caused by her father's incestuous desires. In many ways the emotional patterning in each of those two story types mirrors or echoes that in the other. The first may be represented by Perrault's 'Cendrillon' or 'Cinderella'; the second by Perrault's 'Peau d'Ane' or 'Donkey-Skin'.

In fact both of these 'strands' have two characteristic story forms. The girl persecuted by her stepmother has two distinct stories, which can be contrasted in two Grimm tales, 'Aschenputtle' (the equivalent of Perrault's 'Cendrillon') and 'Einauglein, Zweiauglein und Drei-auglein', 'One-Eye, Two-Eyes and Three-Eyes'. In this book the first of these forms is represented by 'Cendrillon', 'Askenbasken, who Became Queen', 'Ashey Pelt' and 'The Traveller's Cinderella', the second by 'Burenushka, the Little Red Cow'. In many stories, however, such as 'Yeh-hsien', they will be seen to merge.

The story of the girl desired by her father has two characteristic openings. Either the girl flees from her father's advances or – like Cordelia in *King Lear* – she is cast out because she does not sufficiently assert her love for him, often saying that she loves him as much as meat loves salt. The motifs of the 'unnatural father' and 'love like salt' also branch off into other folktale types. The Grimms' 'Allerleirauh' is an example of this sort of Cinderella tale, which is represented in this book by 'Mossycoat', 'Rashin Coatie', 'La Sendraoeula', and 'Dona Labismina'.

There are also male Cinderellas, the most characteristic of which, represented here by 'The Bracket Bull', are the male equivalent of the 'One-Eye, Two-Eyes and Three-Eyes' story.

The fact that the Grimms' collection alone yields three Cinderella variants indicates how popular such tales have been. The three Grimm stories display many longstanding features of the international cycle: 'Aschenputtle' has the persecution by the stepmother and stepsisters, the treasure-giving tree growing from the mother's grave, the helpful animal, the three-fold ball which Aschenputtle can attend only when she has sorted lentils from ashes, the lost slipper, the search for its wearer, the pretence of the stepsisters who mutilate their feet to fit the shoe, only to be unmasked by the song of birds, the recognition and marriage, and, in the Grimms' harsh world, savage retribution on the stepsisters. 'One-Eye, Two-Eyes and Three-Eyes' has the persecution of Two-Eyes by her sisters and mother, her succour by a goat which provides food and drink at her bidding, its discovery and murder through her sisters' spying and spite, the burial of the entrails and growth from them of a magical tree, and the promise of marriage to the girl who can break off a branch (or in many stories, pick fruit) from it; Two-Eyes alone can pass the test, and the tree follows her to her new home. 'Allerleirauh', often translated as 'The Many-Furred Creature' or 'Thousandfurs', has the king who promises his dying wife that he will marry only someone just like her, and becomes determined to marry his own daughter, who demands three special dresses – one as golden as the sun, one as silver as the moon, one as glittering as the stars – before she will consent. He provides the garments and the girl flees in a cloak made from a thousand furs (or rushes, in many stories), and takes a lowly job in a kitchen. Three times she wears her dresses to a ball where a king falls in love with her; she cooks his soup, hiding in it token objects by which she is recognized.

These basic plot structures, and the individual elements of each narrative, can be traced through the world's folk literatures by consulting two key reference works in which folktale plots are analysed and classified: Aarne's and Thompson's *Types of the Folktale* and Thompson's *Motif-Index of Folk-Literature*. These books, the use of which is clarified in Stith Thompson's classic study *The Folktale*, are indispensable to anyone seriously studying the subject.

Using such tools, it is fatally easy to get bogged down in classification and comparison, as if all that mattered in a given narration was the order and nature of the events in it. This is not so. Each version should stand and be considered on its own, as well as for its relation to the 'cycle'. The language, the images, the idiosyncrasies are the expression of the storyteller's creativity and should not take second place to questions of structure. The way in which folktales work – by building up clusters of narrative units, or 'motifs', and then referring these to established patterns of such units, or 'tale types' – has built into it not only a narrative fail-safe, a sort of self-repairing and self-perpetuating mechanism, but also the possibility for endless experiment and assimilation. The tale types that in an index look discrete and separate may fuse and cross-refer in actual telling.

Nevertheless it seems worthwhile here to attempt to describe briefly the main variations of the Cinderella story, and outline its historical development.

Perrault's 'Cendrillon' seems to be a fairly recent, European development of a story which has its roots in the Orient. Anna Birgitta Rooth regards the earliest traceable form of the tale as a basic 'One-Eye, Two-Eyes and Three-Eyes' story, in which mistreated motherless children are supplied with food by a helpful animal which is the reincarnation of the mother. The children are spied on by their step-siblings, and the animal is killed by the stepmother, but its grave, or a tree which grows from its grave, continues to provide the children with food.

This simple story developed into a more complex version in which there was a single focus of attention, a motherless girl, and in which the tree growing from the grave acted – as in Grimm – as a marriage test: only the girl could pick the fruit.

This story in turn assimilated the oriental motif of the object that is lost and found by chance, such as a shoe. To explain why the girl should possess a valuable or beautiful object, the visit to the feast was added, as in 'Yeh-hsien'. In oriental tales the visit to the feast is not the occasion of the girl meeting the prince, which is brought about by the chance finding of the lost object. It is a European development that the feast, ball or church service should also serve as the meeting place, with the consequent flight of the girl and pursuit by the prince.

This crucial change, emphasized by the three-fold visit which is also part of the European tradition, created a new centre of interest in the story, paving the way for the Perrault-type Cinderella story in which the motifs of the earlier story, such as the helpful food-providing animal, the slaying of the animal, the burying of the bones or entrails, and growth of the food-providing tree, are reduced in importance and sometimes dispensed with altogether. What remains is the persecuted stepdaughter, the helpful reincarnated mother, and the tree which gives not food but beautiful clothes in order to lead into the three-fold feast, flight and pursuit, the shoe test and the marriage.

In other words, Rooth agrees with the Aarne–Thompson tale-type index in separating 'Cinderella' (Aarne–Thompson type 510a) and 'One-Eye, Two-Eyes and Three-Eyes' (AT511), while also identifying an intermediate form which has the opening of 'One-Eye, Two-Eyes and Three-Eyes' and the conclusion of 'Cinderella', from which she suggests the Perrault-type 'Cinderella' has developed. This separate development occurred, she reasons, because a cross-fertilization in the Near East and Southern and South-Eastern Europe of the intermediate tale and another tale type, 'The Kind and Unkind Girls' or 'The Spinning Woman by the Spring' (AT480), loosened the bonds between the opening and closing sections, allowing the ending to be made into a tale in its own right. For an example of this intermediate form crossed with 'The Kind and Unkind Girls' in this book, see 'The Poor Girl and her Cow'.

Rooth regards 'The Dress of Gold, of Silver and of Stars' or 'Cap o' Rushes' (AT510b), the type in which the girl flees her father, as having developed in tandem with 'Cinderella', rather than from the same root. Whatever the truth, the types are now closely, and fruitfully, intertwined. In the most usual form of this story, a dying queen extracts a deathbed promise from the king that he will marry only someone who is as beautiful as her, or who can fit her ring, or her clothes. The father decides to marry his daughter, who is the only girl who fits the bill. The daughter asks for three fine dresses, and flees disguised in a wooden skirt, a cape of rushes, or a many-furred coat. She goes into service, makes three incognito visits to a feast in her three dresses, naming token objects when asked who she is or where she comes from. The prince falls sick for love of the unknown girl, and she serves him a meal in which she places a recognition token, usually a ring, and they marry. Stories with the *King Lear* 'Love Like Salt' opening follow a similar course, though the father turns up again at the wedding feast where the girl proves the value of her love by serving up all the meat unsalted and tasteless.

The precise historical arguments and definitions of geographical tradition areas in Anna Birgitta Rooth's formidable study are too complex to rehearse here. Suffice it to say that there are very definite cultural variations. Outside the Orient, where Rooth identifies two separate traditions, the Near Eastern and the Indo-Malayan, 'One-Eye, Two-Eyes and Three-Eyes' is chiefly found in Slavonic and Baltic areas, where it conforms to the Near Eastern pattern. The intermediate type developed in the Near East from which it spread to Europe and Indo-China. The straightforward 'Cinderella' type is a European development of this.

Introduction

Cinderella is so widely known that it is sometimes said to be 'known all over the world'. This is misleading. In fact, the Cinderella cycle is essentially Eur-Asian; it is not native to Africa, Australasia or the Americas. Nevertheless, Cinderella tales have now been reported from all these areas, for wherever the tale has travelled it has been enthusiastically adopted: by the Micmac, Zuni, Piegan and Ojibwa Indians; by the Arabs of North Africa and by such sub-Saharan Africans as the Hausa and the Tonga; by Filipinos and other Indonesians.

Similarly, Cinderella is sometimes described as immeasurably ancient. For instance one of the most provocative and interesting modern writers on the folktale, Jack Zipes, claims in his *Breaking the Magic Spell*: 'Nitschke has demonstrated that Cinderella originated toward the end of the Ice Age.' This is pure claptrap: no such demonstration is possible. The earliest recognizable Cinderella story known to us is the Chinese story of Yeh-hsien, dating in this text from the ninth century A D. The earliest European Cinderella is the 'Cat Cinderella' ('La Gatta Cenerentola') of Basile's *Il Pentamerone* (*Lo Cunto de li Cunte*) published posthumously between 1634 and 1636, though Bonaventure des Periers' *Les Nouvelles Recreations et Joyeux Devis* (1558) contained a tale of the Catskin type of the 1570s. The vast majority of recorded Cinderella tales date from the nineteenth and twentieth centuries.

This is not to say, of course, that similar stories have not been told for countless years – the Chinese story, for instance, seems already battered by oral transmission rather than freshly invented – but it is a bad habit to make assumptions rather than suppositions about matters for which we simply have no direct evidence. The most authoritative statement on the age of the tale is that of Anna Birgitta Rooth in her essay, supplementary to her book-length monograph, 'Tradition Areas in Eurasia'. She writes that 'it is possible to state a minimum age for the tradition of many an area or sub-area. In Indo-China the nineteenth-century tradition has the same special motifs as a version written down in the ninth century. In Iceland the special Icelandic traits were in existence in the thirteenth century. In the Balkans, motifs special for Balkan Cinderella were extant 2000 years ago, etc. This goes to show that each tradition area had its special form of the tale already fixed, often more than 1000 years ago and that the diffusion of the tale must have been prior to this date.' We can assume, then, a certain continuity and longevity of tradition in many areas; but to carry the history back to the late Pleistocene seems unduly rash.

In the twenty-odd Cinderella texts that follow, I have chosen stories with particularly interesting features, or which exhibit some special vitality or narrative skill, rather than ones which will ploddingly exemplify the foregoing sketch of Cinderella's history. The notes to each tale give some background information, but the point of the book is the tales themselves, in all their rich variety. They are stories which succinctly imply a great deal about human relationships and the human imagination, without requiring any single, narrow response. I have avoided any discussion of meaning, symbolism or psychology, in the hope that the reader will bring his or her individual viewpoint to bear on such matters without any clumsy prompting. All I hope is that each reader will at the end of the book understand why the Scottish writer David Toulmin, searching for a way to describe the wonder and strangeness of a rich unexplored house, should write, 'It was all so Cinderella.'

Cendrillon, or, The Little Glass Slipper

Source: Charles Perrault, *Histoires ou Contes du Temps Passé. Avec des Moralitez* (*Contes de ma mère l'oye*), first published 1697; edited by Andrew Lang as *Perrault's Popular Tales*, Oxford, Clarendon Press, 1888. There is a good modern critical edition by Gilbert Rouger, Paris: Classiques Garnier, 1967. Translated by Neil Philip with Nicoletta Simborowski.

Charles Perrault was born in Paris in 1628 and died in 1703. He was a civil servant, and as a member of the Académie Française engaged in the literary affairs of his day. His *Contes* were first published anonymously in the journal *Recueil de pièces curieuses et nouvelles* in the 1690s ('Cendrillon', and most of the prose tales, appeared in 1697, vol. 5, part 4). When they were collected in volume form in 1697, they were attributed not to Perrault, but to his son Pierre Darmancour, then aged eighteen. There are still large areas of uncertainty regarding the tales' authorship and provenance. But it seems fairly certain both that Perrault wrote them, and that his source or sources lay in oral tradition.

Whatever his sources, Perrault was not concerned to record or protect them. He used them as raw material for his own talent, confidently shaping the rough spoken tales into smooth written ones. His dry courtly ironies, turning naive household tales into sophisticated short stories, spoke to the temper of his day and – because of the perceived authority of print – fixed the form of those tales for every generation since. Much that we accept as basic to Cinderella – even the miraculously transformed rat and pumpkin – we owe to Perrault's literary imagination. The fairy godmother is a polite substitution for the mother reincarnated as a helpful animal.

Perrault's tales founded a literary genre. The taste for fairy tales was fed by such writers as Madame d'Aulnoy, Madame Leprince de Beaumont and the Comte de Caylus. Madame d'Aulnoy gave us, in 1698, a parallel Cinderella, 'Finette Cendron'. But her tale has never attained the widespread popularity of Perrault's 'Cendrillon'.

'Cendrillon' has been translated into English many times, first by Robert Samber in 1729, a version reprinted in the Opies' *Classic Fairy Tales*. It has also been used as the basis of countless retellings. The new translation given here aims to catch some of the austerity of Perrault's formal yet simple and concise prose, to amend at least in part for the soppy sentimentality of many of these retellings. Perrault is an astringent writer.

We cannot, however, view 'Cendrillon' as simply Perrault's creation. We know that the tale has a long history in various forms both before and after he put pen to paper. Interestingly, his version did not stifle the tale in France: *Le Conte Populaire Français* by Paul Delarue and Marie-Louise Tenèze lists a rich haul of over a hundred French variants. 'Cendrillon' is best seen as one version among many. It stands at the head of this book as a familiar setting-off point for a strange journey, rather than as a model towards which the other texts strive, or from which they fall away.

THERE WAS ONCE a man who took for his second wife the most haughty, stuck-up woman you ever saw. She had two daughters of her own type, just like her in everything. The husband for his part had a young daughter, but she was gentle and sweet-natured, taking after her mother, who was the best person in the world.

The wedding was barely over when the stepmother let her temper show; she couldn't bear the young girl's goodness, for it made her daughters seem yet more hateful. She gave her the vilest household chores: it was she who cleaned the dishes and the stairs, she who scrubbed Madam's chamber, and the chambers of those little madams, her daughters: she slept at the top of the house in an attic, on a shabby mattress, while her sisters had panelled boudoirs, with beds of the latest fashion, and mirrors in which they could study themselves from head to toe. The poor girl suffered it all patiently, and didn't dare complain to her father, who would have scolded her, because he was completely under the woman's sway.

When she had done her work, she would retire to the chimney corner and sit in the cinders, so that they commonly called her Cinderbutt; though the younger sister, who wasn't quite so rude as the elder, called her Cinderella; and despite everything Cinderella in her rags was still a hundred times prettier than her sisters for all their sumptuous clothes.

It happened that the King's son gave a Ball, to which he asked all the quality; our two misses were also asked, as they cut quite a dash in the district. They were thrilled, and kept themselves very busy choosing the clothes and hairstyles which would show them off best; a new worry for Cinderella because it was she who ironed her sisters' petticoats and pleated their ruffles: and they couldn't talk of anything but clothes. 'Myself,' said the elder, 'I'll wear my red velvet gown with the English trimming.' 'As for me,' said the younger, 'I'll just wear a simple skirt, but to make up for that I'll have my shawl with the golden flowers, and my diamond cummerbund, which isn't the plainest ever made.'

They sent for an expert to adjust their two-layered head-dresses, and bought beauty spots; they asked Cinderella for her advice, because she had such good taste. Cinderella gave them every possible help, and offered to do their hair herself, which they were pleased to accept. But while she combed, they said to her, 'Cinderella, wouldn't you like to go to the Ball?'

Cinderella sighed. 'You're making fun of me, ladies, that's not my place.'

'You're right. People would have a good laugh to see a Cinderbutt at the Ball.'

Anyone else but Cinderella would have tangled their hair, but she was good, and she did it to perfection.

The sisters went nearly two days without eating, they were so excited, and they broke more than a dozen corset-laces pulling them tight to get a wasp waist, and they were always at the mirror.

At last, the happy day arrived, and they set off. Cinderella stared after them as long as she could, and when she could no longer see them, she began to cry. Her Godmother, who saw her weeping, asked her what she wanted.

'I want . . . I want . . .' She cried so hard she couldn't finish.

Her Godmother, who was a Fairy, said, 'You want to go to the Ball, isn't that it?'

'Yes,' sighed Cinderella.

'Well, if you're a good girl, I shall send you,' said her Godmother. She took her into her own room and told her, 'Go into the garden and bring me a pumpkin.'

Cinderella went straight and picked the finest she could find, and took it to her Godmother, without the least idea how a pumpkin could help her go to the Ball. Her Godmother scooped it out to a hollow

skin, then tapped it with her wand, and the pumpkin was instantly turned into a beautiful gilded carriage. Then she looked in the mouse-trap, where she found six live mice. She told Cinderella to lift the trap door a little, and as each mouse escaped, she struck it with her wand, and the mouse was straightway changed into a handsome horse. They made a fine set of six horses, all a lovely mouse-coloured dapple grey.

As her Godmother was having difficulty finding something she could turn into a coachman, Cinderella said, 'I'll go and see if there is a rat in the rat-trap, and we can make a coachman of him.'

'Good idea,' said her Godmother, 'go and see.'

Cinderella brought her the rat-trap, in which there were three fat rats. The Fairy chose the one with the finest whiskers, and with a touch transformed him into a portly coachman, with the most lavish moustache you ever saw.

'Now,' she said, 'go into the garden, and you'll find six lizards behind the watering can. Bring them to me.'

No sooner had she fetched them in than her Godmother changed them into six footmen, who climbed up behind the carriage in their brocade livery, and clung there as if they had done nothing else all their lives.

The Fairy said to Cinderella, 'Well, now you can go to the Ball. Aren't you happy?'

'Yes, but do I have to go like this, in tatters?'

Her Godmother just touched her with her wand, and her clothes changed into garments of gold and silver cloth, embroidered all over with jewels. Then she gave her a pair of glass slippers, the prettiest in the world.

When she was ready, she got into the carriage; but her Godmother warned her on no account to stay after midnight, for if she stayed at the Ball one moment longer, her carriage would turn back into a pumpkin, the horses into mice, the footmen into lizards, and her old clothes would look just like before.

She promised her Godmother that she would leave the Ball before midnight without fail, and set off, beside herself with joy.

When the Prince was told that a grand Princess had arrived whom nobody knew, he ran out to welcome her, and gave her his hand to step down from the carriage, and took her himself into the room where the people were. They all fell silent; the dancing ceased; the violins stopped playing; all eyes were on the rare beauty of this unknown woman.

The only noise was a confused murmuring, 'Oh! she's beautiful!'

Even the King, ancient as he was, couldn't stop looking at her, and whispering to the Queen that it was a long while since he'd seen anyone so lovely, so beautiful.

All the ladies studied her hair and her clothes, to have copies made the next day, if they could find such gorgeous materials, and such skilful dressmakers.

The Prince led her to the seat of honour, and afterwards took her on to the dance floor; she danced with such grace, everyone admired her yet more. There was a splendid supper, but the Prince couldn't eat a thing, he was so wrapped up in her.

She went and sat near her sisters, and showed them every civility; she gave them some of the oranges and lemons the Prince had given her, which surprised them very much, for they didn't recognize her at all. As they chatted, Cinderella heard the chimes mark a quarter to twelve. She immediately curtseyed to the company, and left as fast as she could.

When she got home, she found her Godmother, and after thanking her, told her that she wanted very much to go to the Ball again on the next day, because the Prince had begged her to come. Whilst she was telling her Godmother everything that had happened at the Ball, the two sisters knocked at the door, and Cinderella let them in.

'What a long time you've been,' she told them, yawning and rubbing her eyes, and stretching as if she had just woken up; though she hadn't had a sleepy thought since they left home.

'If you'd been at the Ball,' said one of the sisters, 'you wouldn't have been wearied: there was the most beautiful Princess there, the loveliest you could ever see; she was so kind to us, and gave us oranges and lemons.'

Cinderella was beside herself with joy: she asked what the Princess's name was, but they told her that nobody knew, that the Prince was in despair, and would give the whole world to know who she was. Cinderella smiled and said, 'Was she really so beautiful? Gracious, you are lucky! Can't I see her? Oh dear! Miss Javotte, lend me your yellow dress, the one you wear every day.'

'Lend my dress to a grimy Cinderbutt?' said Miss Javotte. 'One would have to be stark mad, to be sure.'

Cinderella knew very well she would refuse, and she was quite happy, because she would have been in an embarrassing fix if her sister had really agreed to lend her the dress.

The next day the two sisters went to the Ball, and Cinderella too, still more grandly dressed than the first time. The Prince was always by her, and never stopped talking sweet nothings; the young lady wasn't at all bored, and forgot what her Godmother told her, with the result that she heard the first stroke of midnight when she thought it was still only eleven. She jumped up and fled, as nimbly as a doe. The Prince followed her. He couldn't catch her, but she did drop one of her glass slippers, which the Prince picked up tenderly.

Cinderella got home all puffed out, no carriage, no flunkeys, in her grubby clothes, with nothing left of her magnificence save a single little slipper, the mate of the one she dropped.

The palace guards were asked if they saw the Princess leave. They said they saw no one leave but a badly dressed girl who looked more like a peasant than a lady.

When the two sisters returned from the Ball, Cinderella asked them if they had enjoyed themselves again, and if the beautiful lady had come; they told her yes, but she had fled as midnight struck, so hastily that she had let fall one of her little glass slippers, the prettiest in the world. The Prince had picked it up, and done nothing but look at it for the rest of the Ball. He was certainly head-over-heels in love with the lovely owner of the little slipper.

They were telling the truth. A few days later, the Prince had it cried to the sound of trumpets that he would marry the girl whose foot fitted the slipper. He started by trying all the Princesses, then the Duchesses, and all the Court: but it was no use. The slipper was brought to the two sisters, who tried everything to force their feet into the slipper, but they couldn't manage it. Cinderella, who was watching, and who recognized her own slipper, laughed and said, 'Let me see if it fits me.'

Her sisters burst out laughing, and jeered at her. The gentleman in charge of the slipper looked closely at Cinderella, and finding her extremely attractive, said she was right, because he'd been told to try all the girls. He made Cinderella sit down, and putting the slipper on her tiny foot, he saw it slipped on easily, and fitted as perfectly, as if it was made of wax. The sisters were astonished, but even more so when Cinderella took the other little slipper from her pocket and put it on her foot. Then the Godmother came and touched Cinderella's clothes with her wand, making them turn into garments even more stunning than all the others.

So the two sisters recognized her as the beautiful lady they had seen at the Ball. They threw themselves at her feet and asked forgiveness for all the harsh treatment they had made her suffer. Cinderella raised them up, and kissed them, and forgave them with all her heart, and asked them to love her always.

She was taken to the Prince dressed as she was, and he thought her even more beautiful than ever, and a few days later he married her. Cinderella, who was as good as she was beautiful, took her sisters to live in the palace, and married them the same day to two great lords of the court.

Moral

Beauty in woman is a very rare treasure:
Of it we can never tire.
But what's worth more, a priceless pleasure,
Is charm, which we must all admire.

That wise instructress, the Godmother,
While dressing her fit for a Queen
Was giving her power to charm another;
That is what this story means.

The Cinderella Story

Ladies, better than teased-up hair is,
To win a heart, and conquer a Ball.
Charm is the true gift of the fairies;
Without it you've nothing; with it, all.

Another moral

It is no doubt a great advantage
To have shrewdness, wit and courage
To be well born, with every sense
And have all sorts of other talents
Which Heaven gives you for your share
But with or without them, when all is said
They'll never help you get ahead
Unless to spread your talents further
You've a willing godmother, or godfather.

Yeh-hsien

Source: Arthur Waley, 'The Chinese Cinderella Story', *Folk-Lore* 58, London, The Folklore Society, 1947. Translated by Arthur Waley from Tuan Ch'êng-shih, *Yu Yang Tsa Tsu* (*Miscellany of Forgotten Lore*), AD 850–860, where it is recorded from the narration of Li Shih-yüan.

'Yeh-hsien' is the earliest recorded version of the Cinderella story. It was written down in this form by a Chinese official with an interest in out-of-the-way information, Tuan Ch'êng-shih, who lived from about AD 800 to 863. His source for the story was 'Li Shih-yüan, who has been in the service of my family for a long while. He was himself originally a man from the caves of Yung-chou and remembers many strange things of the South.' Yung-chou, the translator Arthur Waley tells us, 'corresponds to the modern Nan-ning, in the province of Kwangsi, about 100 miles north of the frontiers of Annam'.

Elements found in this early record recur in Annamese and Cham narratives collected in the nineteenth century (see 'Kajong and Haloek', p. 21) as well as in later Chinese versions, such as that entitled 'Cinderella' in Wolfram Eberhard's *Folktales of China*. This collection of Eberhard's, with his *Typen Chinesischer Volksmärchen*, makes a good starting point for study of the Chinese tale, though it predates the great, ambiguous waves of Red Chinese enthusiasm for folktale collecting.

The Chinese Cinderella story is the subject of Nai-Tung Ting's monograph *The Cinderella Cycle in China and Indonesia*; commentaries on this first recorded version can be found in Arthur Waley's article and, together with an earlier translation, in R. D. Jameson's *Three Lectures on Chinese Folklore*.

Little is known about the ethnic or linguistic basis of the cave-dwelling people Tuan Ch'êng-shih terms 'aborigines of Hsi-yüan' and to whom he attaches the story of 'Yeh-hsien'. Waley notes that the girl's name is written with Chinese characters meaning 'Leaf-limit'.

The most noteworthy aspect of this tale for an audience conditioned by Perrault is the dislocation between the loss of the shoe and its finding. This chance finding is common in oriental Cinderellas; it recalls the story of the Egyptian courtesan Rhodopis told by the Greek historian Strabo in the first century B C. When she was bathing in the Nile, an eagle carried her shoe to Memphis and dropped it in the King's lap; he searched for the shoe's owner and married her.

An interesting children's picture-book version of this story, *Yeh-Shen* by Ai-Ling Louie, illustrated by the Chinese artist Ed Young, was published in 1982: the author bases her tale on the early text, but remembered it also from her grandmother's narration.

AMONG THE PEOPLE of the south there is a tradition that before the Ch'in and Han dynasties there was a cave-master called Wu. The aborigines called the place the Wu cave. He married two wives. One wife died. She had a daughter called Yeh-hsien, who from childhood was intelligent and good at making pottery on the wheel. Her father loved her. After some years the father died, and she was ill-treated by her step-mother, who always made her collect firewood in dangerous places and draw water from deep pools. She once got a fish about two inches long, with red fins and golden eyes. She put it into a bowl of water. It grew bigger every day, and after she had changed the bowl several times she could find no bowl big enough for it, so she threw it into the back pond. Whatever food was left over from meals she put into the water to feed it. When she came to the pond, the fish always exposed its head and pillowed it on the bank; but when anyone else came, it did not come out. The step-mother knew about this, but when she watched for it, it did not once appear. So she tricked the girl, saying, 'Haven't you worked hard! I am going to give you a new dress.' She then made the girl change out of her tattered clothing. Afterwards she sent her to get water from another spring and reckoning that it was several hundred leagues, the step-mother at her leisure put on her daughter's clothes, hid a sharp blade up her sleeve, and went to the pond. She called to the fish. The fish at once put its head out, and she chopped it off and killed it. The fish was now more than ten feet long. She served it up and it tasted twice as good as an ordinary fish. She hid the bones under the dung-hill. Next day, when the girl came to the pond, no fish appeared. She howled with grief in the open countryside, and suddenly there appeared a man with his hair loose over his shoulders and coarse clothes. He came down from the sky. He

consoled her saying, 'Don't howl! Your step-mother has killed the fish and its bones are under the dung. You go back, take the fish's bones and hide them in your room. Whatever you want, you have only to pray to them for it. It is bound to be granted.' The girl followed his advice, and was able to provide herself with gold, pearls, dresses and food whenever she wanted them.

When the time came for the cave-festival, the step-mother went, leaving the girl to keep watch over the fruit-trees in the garden. She waited till the step-mother was some way off, and then went herself, wearing a cloak of stuff spun from kingfisher feathers and shoes of gold. Her step-sister recognized her and said to the step-mother, 'That's very like my sister.' The step-mother suspected the same thing. The girl was aware of this and went away in such a hurry that she lost one shoe. It was picked up by one of the people of the cave. When the step-mother got home, she found the girl asleep, with her arms round one of the trees in the garden, and thought no more about it.

This cave was near to an island in the sea. On this island was a kingdom called T'o-han. Its soldiers had subdued twenty or thirty other islands and it had a coast-line of several thousand leagues. The cave-man sold the shoe in T'o-han, and the ruler of T'o-han got it. He told those about him to put it on; but it was an inch too small even for the one among them that had the smallest foot. He ordered all the women in his kingdom to try it on; but there was not one that it fitted. It was light as down and made no noise even when treading on stone. The king of T'o-han thought the cave-man had got it unlawfully. He put him in prison and tortured him, but did not end by finding out where it had come from. So he threw it down at the wayside. Then they went everywhere through all the people's houses and arrested them. If there was a woman's shoe, they arrested them and told the king of T'o-han. He thought it strange, searched the inner-rooms and found Yeh-hsien. He made her put on the shoe, and it was true.

Yeh-hsien then came forward, wearing her cloak spun from halcyon feathers and her shoes. She was as beautiful as a heavenly being. She now began to render service to the king, and he took the fish-bones and Yeh-hsien, and brought them back to his country.

The step-mother and step-sister were shortly afterwards struck by flying stones, and died. The cave people were sorry for them and buried them in a stone-pit, which was called the Tomb of the Distressed Women. The men of the cave made mating-offerings there; any girl they prayed for there, they got. The king of T'o-han, when he got back to his kingdom made Yeh-hsien his chief wife. The first year the king was very greedy and by his prayers to the fish-bones got treasures and jade without limit. Next year, there was no response, so the king buried the fish-bones on the sea-shore. He covered them with a hundred bushels of pearls and bordered them with gold. Later there was a mutiny of some soldiers who had been conscripted and their general opened (the hiding-place) in order to make better provision for his army. One night they (the bones) were washed away by the tide.

Kajong and Haloek

Source: A. Landes, *Contes Tjames, traduits et annotés*, Saigon, Imprimerie Coloniale, 1887. Translated from the French by Nicoletta Simborowski and Neil Philip.

Like many texts of the nineteenth century, 'Kajong and Haloek' was collected by a colonial administrator. It was written down for Landes by a Cham called Mul Tjoek – the Chams being an Indonesian people living in Cambodia and Vietnam. Mul Tjoek wrote this and other stories in Cham, and then explained them in Annamese; Landes then translated into French, aiming for strict literal accuracy, save for the introduction of pronouns. The story may be compared with a similar text in A. Landes's *Contes et Legendes Annamites*, summarized as tale 68 in Marian Cox's *Cinderella*. Landes suggests that 'Alwah' in this tale may be a corruption of Allah, and notes that the *moekya* tree bears a fruit with a penetrating odour, of which the seeds resemble the female silhouette.

The beginning of this narrative is quite confusing; it should be borne in mind that Kajong is the adopted daughter, and Haloek is the true daughter.

ONCE THERE WERE two daughters, Haloek and Kajong, one the true daughter, the other adopted. No one knew which of the two was the older, which the younger, for they were the same age. The mother was anguished in her heart to see them equal, not knowing which was the older, which the younger.

The mother told Haloek to call Kajong 'older sister'. Haloek replied that Kajong and she were equals, that her mother could do what she liked and she would consent, but that she would not call Kajong 'older sister'. So the mother ordered Kajong to call Haloek 'older sister', but Kajong wouldn't agree. So then she wanted Kajong to call Haloek 'older sister' one day, and 'miss' the next.

Haloek told her mother, if Kajong must call her 'miss', then she should call her 'miss', and if Kajong must call her 'older sister', then she should call her 'older sister', but to call her 'older sister' one day and 'miss' the next – she would be shamed in front of all their relations. So the mother took baskets, gave them to Haloek and Kajong, and told them to catch fish. If Kajong caught more fish than Haloek she would be the senior; if Haloek caught more fish then Kajong it would be she who was the senior.

The two sisters went fishing, and they came to a big pool in which there were many fish; all the fish you can find, every kind of fish was in that pool. Kajong went down into the water and started to fish. But as for Haloek she didn't care to go into the water to fish. Kajong caught thirteen fish. So Haloek went into the water to fish. Kajong had half a basket-full. Haloek only caught ten *krwak*. Kajong left her basket of fish and, tired, lay down on the bank.

Haloek fished by the side of Kajong's basket. With a snatch here and a snatch there, she stole Kajong's fish, till she had many and Kajong only a few. When Kajong came back she asked Haloek: 'Who's taken the fish from my basket?' Haloek said it wasn't her. Kajong said nothing more; she knew it was Haloek who had stolen her fish. Kajong thought sad thoughts to herself; if she went home, her foster mother would thrash her. She fished again, but only caught a *tjarok*. Haloek went home first, Kajong after. Kajong took her *tjarok* and put it in a well, to look after it so it would be her brother; as for the three *tjaklek* fish she had also caught, she took those to the house. Kajong thought that the *tjarok* she had caught was lonely like her, that's why she nourished it, to be her brother. As for the three *tjaklek* fish they weren't lonely like her, so she took them to her foster mother.

The foster mother, seeing that she had caught less fish, ordered her to call Haloek 'older sister'. She agreed to call her 'older sister', and as for telling how Haloek stole her fish, she didn't tell her foster mother that.

Her mother told her to tend the goats which she had just bought. When Kajong went to mind the goats, she took them past the well in which she was looking after her fish. She went to see the fish, and told him: 'O *tjarok*! your older sister has come to see you: I caught you and saw you were lonely like me, that's why I had pity on you. Now I'm raising you to be my younger brother.'

That's how she talked to the *tjarok*, then she tended the goats. At noon she shut up the goats, took some rice and carried it to the fish for it to eat. She took the rice to the *tjarok* and told him: 'O *tjarok*! come and eat rice, come and gather the rice I am throwing.' Kajong took the rice and threw it in the well for the *tjarok* to eat. Kajong ate her rice by the well with the fish, and then went back to the house. Each day she took her rice and went to eat it with the fish.

In the following days when she took her rice and went to eat it with the fish, she would call it to eat, and the fish who knew her heard the call and came to the surface to eat with her. For a month she always went to eat with the fish. Haloek, seeing her take the rice away, followed her and spied on her. She saw that while Kajong ate she called the fish, which rose and ate with her. Then Haloek went back to the house.

The next day Kajong took the goats to pasture. The goats ate the cotton, and Kajong was busy gathering the flock, and didn't go to see the fish. Haloek was at home, she took rice and went to eat it by the well with the fish. She called to the fish to come and eat and the fish heard. The fish thought it was Kajong calling, and surfaced. Haloek grabbed it and took it to the house. She cut the fish in two, cooked it with *nuoc mam* and ate it all up.

Haloek ate the fish without saying anything to her mother or Kajong. Next day, Kajong took rice and went to eat by the well but she didn't see the fish again. She searched the well but she didn't find him there any more.

Kajong cried sadly, thinking that she had no parents, but she had a fish which she was raising as her younger brother, and now she didn't know what pitiless person had stolen him. Every day she consoled herself with the fish, and now someone had stolen him and she was all alone. She cried night and day.

That night she saw the fish in a dream; he said: 'O Kajong, older sister, don't cry any more, my sister! As for me, she who is called Haloek ate me while you tended the goats. She brought rice and called me to eat, she caught me, took me to the house, cooked me with *nuoc mam* and ate me. As for my bones, she put them in a bamboo tube and buried it by the water jar. If you love me, take my bones, put them in a coconut shell, and bury them at a crossroads, so that when you go to tend the goats I can see my sister's face. If you do that, you can come and see me all the time.'

The fish said that to Kajong, and as he spoke he cried. Kajong woke up crying and alone, on her matting in the middle of the night. Next morning she dug by the water jar and found a bamboo tube there. She looked in the tube and found the fish's bones. Kajong cried, then she took the bones, put them in a coconut shell and went to bury them at the crossroads. She said: 'O my brother! as you told me in my dream I have taken your bones and I have buried them here so that coming and going to tend the goats I can visit you to soothe my heart. For I am all alone, my brother. I have no mother, I have no father, my lot is truly miserable, O my brother! I've no brother any more. As for my foster mother: how many times has she had pity on me?'

So Kajong spoke to the bones, and all the while her tears ran freely. Then she went back to the house. Next day she took her goats to graze. On the way she went to see the fish's bones, and found a gold shoe at the place where she had buried them. A crow had carried off one shoe and let it fall in the king's palace, where the king found it. Kajong found the other. The bones that Kajong had buried had changed into the shoes.

Kajong took the shoe and hid it, then she fetched the goats home. After two or three days the king sent a letter to every village in the land, saying that all the young girls, large and small, should go to the palace to try on the king's shoe, the shoe which the crow had picked up and which the king had found. If anyone could put the shoe on, and it fitted her foot, if it was neither too large nor too small, but just right, well, the king would marry her.

In every village throughout the land those with daughters told them to go to the king's palace to try the shoe that the king had found. The mother told Haloek to go first, but as for Kajong, she wouldn't let her go.

Kajong thought about it all, was sad at heart, and cried. Her adoptive mother, seeing her crying, took a tangle of thread and told her to unravel it, then she could go to the palace to try the shoe like the others. But Kajong didn't unravel the thread, she didn't do anything but cry. The lord of the sky saw her crying so sadly, and he sent ants to crawl in the thread. The ants crawled in the tangle and separated it all. Kajong took the thread and gave it to her foster mother.

Then the mother took a measure of sesame and a measure of maize and told Kajong to pour them in a sieve, to sort them out, and to put the sesame on one side and the maize on the other. When she had sorted them, she could go with the others.

Half of Kajong was crying, the other half was separating the sesame and the maize. Lord Alwah saw her crying so sadly, he told all the birds of the forest, the termites, the ants, the scorpions, the centipedes, the yellow cockroaches and the red cockroaches to go and help Kajong collect and sort. They sorted out all the sesame and the maize.

Kajong's foster mother then let her go to the king's palace like the others to try the shoe the king had found. Kajong prepared some betel-leaves and folded them in her handkerchief, she put on a *langouti* and set off alone; she was all alone, and arrived at the palace after the others. She went straight to the place where the shoe that she had found was hidden. She took the golden shoe and put it in her handkerchief, then she set off alone, and as she walked, she cried, thinking that the others had gone together in a group: why was it her fate to be alone?

She arrived at the king's palace but didn't dare try the shoe with the others, and stayed hidden behind the palace. As for the rich girls with fathers, they were in the palace vying to get their foot into the shoe the king had found.

All the girls who were in the palace were trying to get their foot into the shoe, but they couldn't. The king asked: 'Of all those who tried the shoe, didn't it fit anyone?' The people replied: 'No one.' The king asked: 'Has everyone tried?' The people replied: 'There is still Kajong who is behind the palace.' The king said: 'Tell her to come in and try.'

The servants fetched Kajong into the palace to try the shoe, she tried it and it fitted her foot just so. The king ordered his servants to take her and have her bathed, and then bring her back to the palace so that he could marry her.

In the middle of the night the king asked Kajong: 'Have you a mother and a father?' She replied: 'My mother and father died when I was a child when I was just starting to walk. I saw my mother, but I never saw my father plain, I was too young. Now I live with my foster mother.' The king took the shoe which he had found, and looked at it. He asked her: 'Have you a shoe like this?' Kajong replied: 'The shoe I found is just like that which the king found.' She showed it to him, the king took it and compared it with the other and saw they were the same. He said: 'It was truly your fate to be my wife, O Kajong!'

All the girls who had tried on the shoe but had been unsuccessful went back home. Haloek returned home and told her mother how from the whole country, from all the villages, people came in their thousands, so many as to crush the grass and beat down the forests, the girls lovely as the night-spirit that follows the full moon, their breasts round as Ra-Pabwak, and not one did the shoe fit; then Kajong came last of all and put the shoe on. Now she was to become the king's wife.

Haloek's mother said bitterly: 'So, my real daughter is not to marry the king and my foster daughter is to marry him!' She went off to tell the king some lie and ask to have Kajong back home. She went to the king's palace. The king asked: 'What does that woman want?' She replied falsely: 'As dust on Your Majesty's holy feet, I come to speak with Your Majesty: I beg you to let Kajong come back home for two or three days, then I will bring her back to you again. If I enter a new home without my foster daughter, I will be extremely sad. Well, my Lord?' The king said: 'So be it! If you want to take Kajong home, take her, but bring her back within a few days.'

The king ordered Kajong to dress in her fine clothes and to go home with her foster mother. Kajong put on her fine clothes and went home with her foster mother.

When they arrived it was dark. The mother and Haloek took rice and ate in the house, but they left Kajong outside. Haloek and her mother did not even call her to taste a mouthful, they ate in the house and shut the door.

Kajong thought about it all sadly. If this was my real mother, would she be annoyed that I was to marry the king? But a foster mother is not flesh and blood. That night Kajong went to bed without eating anything, nor did they give her a mat to sleep on. She slept on a bamboo-screen.

The following morning, Haloek and her mother made up a tale to trick Kajong. Haloek took Kajong to pick coconuts. When they had gone to pick coconuts, she treacherously persuaded Kajong to climb up the coco palm. Kajong climbed up the coco palm and Haloek stayed at the foot; then she took her hatchet and started to cut the tree down. Kajong leapt on to another coco palm, crying: 'Haloek! What are you doing? How can you have the heart to be so treacherous towards me?' Haloek took her hatchet and chopped at the tree where Kajong had leapt. Kajong said, weeping: 'Oh Haloek! You really are determined to kill me! I am an orphan, I have no mother nor father, your mother nurtured me as her own daughter, and now you and your mother dare to behave like this?'

Haloek set to, hacking at the coco palm. Kajong cried out to her:
'Oh, Haloek! When you go home, tell your mother to take you to wed
my husband, I know you!'

Kajong said these words and when she saw that the coco palm was
about to fall, threw herself into a lake that was next to the tree. She was
transformed into a golden turtle and stayed in the lake.

Haloek went back home and told her mother that she had persuaded
Kajong to climb up a coco palm, that she had chopped down the tree
and it had come down and that Kajong had fallen in the lake and was
dead. Mother and daughter were exultant. The mother led her daughter
to the palace. She went into the palace and said to the king: 'Holy dust
on Your Majesty's feet, Kajong ran away from me, I have been unable
to find her, I bring you my real daughter, Haloek, for you to marry.'
The king said: 'So be it! Since you bring your daughter in place of
Kajong, that is how it shall be.' The mother went back home and
Haloek stayed in the king's palace and was his wife in place of Kajong.
But the king was sad, he missed Kajong and could not sleep.

The king told his servants to take him hunting deer and roebuck.
The servants led the king to the lake where Kajong had flung herself
from the top of the coco palm and had been transformed into a golden
turtle. The king was sad, haunted by memories, he did not know what
to do. He stopped his servants for a rest beside the lake and ordered
them to sound its depths.

The servants sounded the lake and caught a golden turtle. The king
clasped the turtle to his bosom and carried it back home. He did not

want to hunt any longer. The king took the turtle and placed it in a golden basin to look after it. He went off for a walk, so Haloek took the golden turtle, cooked it and ate it. She tossed the shell behind the house and from the shell there grew a bamboo shoot.

When the king came back, he went to see the turtle and found it had disappeared. He asked Haloek if she had seen the golden turtle. She replied that she had not. The king then sent for his astrologers to search for it by divination. Then Haloek admitted the truth, saying that she was pregnant, that she had fancied the turtle and had killed it in order to eat it. The king did not say anything to her.

Two or three days later, the king went for a walk behind the house and saw the bamboo shoot springing, and he felt pleasure in his heart and went to touch it and wanted it for his own enjoyment. The king went off to walk again and Haloek picked the bamboo shoot, cooked it and ate it. When the king came back from his walk, he went to see the shoot and found it had disappeared.

The king questioned Haloek and she told him she was pregnant and fancied the bamboo shoot and had eaten it. The king said nothing, but Haloek was not pregnant, she was lying to the king. The king had not slept with her.

The husks of the bamboo shoot were transformed into a *bêk* bird which went and perched, moaning, before the king's palace. When the king heard this *bêk* moaning, he was gripped with sorrow and said the following words: 'If you really are Kajong, come and perch in my sleeve.' The *bêk* flew into the king's sleeve. The king took the bird and kept it. Two or three days later, the king went out for a walk and Haloek, who was left behind at home, took the *bêk*, cooked it and ate it. She threw the feathers on the path outside the king's palace. From these feathers was born a *moekya*.

When the king returned to the palace, he could not see the *bêk* any more and asked Haloek if she had seen it. She said: 'As it flew by, it fell into a pot of soup and perished there; I had put it aside but the dogs carried it off.' Again the king said nothing.

The king pined after the *bêk*. Now, from the *bêk* feathers which Haloek had thrown on to the path, a great *moekya* tree grew. The *moekya* bore just one fruit and when this fruit was ripe it acquired a unique perfume. Whoever passed beneath the tree lifted their eyes to see it, but the fruit was invisible.

An old Annamite woman was off to sell *ratjam* and passed beneath the tree. The ripe fruit filled the air with its scent. The old woman lifted her eyes to the *moekya* and saw the ripe fruit. She said: 'If only I could have that fruit to eat! Isn't it fine!' At that point the fruit fell off the tree. The old woman picked it up, put it in her basket and took it home, where she added it to her rice pot. The old woman went off to sell *ratjam* and left the house empty. She had neither daughter nor granddaughter. Kajong emerged from the *moekya* fruit and made rice appear, and tea, betel, *arec* and all kinds of cake, and this she left in the Annamite woman's house, and then went back into the *moekya* fruit.

When the old woman got back from selling her *ratjam*, she saw the rice on the plate and the cakes in the basket. She said: 'Who can have brought me this rice and these cakes? Is it someone who wishes to put an evil spell on me?' She made a wish and ate some rice and some cakes without coming to any harm. For two or three days the same thing happened. When the old woman went to sell *ratjam*, on her return she found rice and cakes, all left there ready for her. Finally, the old woman hid one day and saw a very beautiful young girl bringing her rice and cakes.

The old woman ran and grasped Kajong by the hand. Kajong began to laugh. The old woman asked her: 'All this time, who brought me rice and cakes?' Kajong said: 'It was me.' The old woman said: 'Where do you come from when you bring me rice and cakes?' Kajong replied: 'I live in the *moekya* fruit which you picked up and which you put in the rice jar.'

The old woman went into the house and looked at the *moekya* fruit, but she only saw an empty peel. She realized that Kajong had supernatural powers and really had come out of the *moekya*.

Kajong ordered the old Annamite woman to invite the king to her house. 'If he asks you why, tell him that you are having a feast.' The old woman replied: 'With such a wretched home, what will we do when the king accepts and arrives?' Kajong replied: 'Just go. When you come back, you will find a beautiful home.' The old Annamite woman went off to invite the king.

The old woman arrived at the king's palace. The dogs barked. The servants asked: 'Who is calling at this hour?' The woman answered: 'It is me.' They said: 'What have you come for?' She replied: 'I have come to invite the king to a feast.' The servants went to inform the king. The king told his servants to get a palanquin to take him to the old Annamite woman's feast. When the servants carried the king from the palace, there was a carpet that stretched from the great door of the palace right to the old woman's house. The king rode in his palanquin to the main door of the old woman's house and saw that it had been filled with cakes.

When the old woman saw how beautiful her house had become, she was astonished. It was Kajong who had made the cakes appear in the house. When the king arrived, he got down and went into the house. Kajong told the old woman to take a basket of the cakes she had produced and offer them to the king. The king ate these cakes and realized that they were exactly like the ones that Kajong used to make. He was gripped by sorrow and stopped eating. He asked the old woman: 'Who made these cakes?' The woman answered: 'I do not know. There are lots of people, I do not know who made these cakes.'

The king chewed some betel from the old woman's basket and realized it tasted exactly like the betel Kajong used to prepare. He started groaning and Kajong groaned too. When the king heard Kajong's groans he went into the old woman's house, saw Kajong and kissed her and wept. The king was sorry for Kajong as she was an orphan. Kajong wept too. The king gave gold and silver to the old Annamite woman to repay her for her services and took Kajong back to the palace. When Haloek saw her, she was deeply troubled. However, she pretended not to be and said: 'So you are back, Kajong!' Kajong said: 'Yes.' Haloek said: 'I came to take your place at the king's side. Do you suppose an outsider would have done as much?'

Kajong then told the king everything her foster mother had done to her, and how Haloek had made her climb the coco palm and had cut the tree down so that she fell into the lake where she had become a turtle. Kajong told the king the whole story.

The following day, Haloek came to talk with Kajong. She asked her: 'How do you keep your skin so white?' Kajong replied jokingly that she heated water in a cauldron and when it was boiling, threw herself in, and that was why she was so white. Haloek wanted to be like her, so she heated a cauldron of water and when the water was boiling, threw herself in, and she was scalded and died. Kajong ordered the servants to pull her out, to cut up the body and pickle it. Then she ordered them to take the jar of salt meat to her foster mother, and if she asked what it was, to tell her it was the salt fish that Haloek had ordered them to take to her and to say that Haloek had begged her to come and visit.

The servants took the salt meat to the mother and said what Kajong had ordered them to say. The mother went to visit Haloek but when she arrived and entered the palace, she saw Kajong. Her eyes were dazzled and she said: 'Is it true that you sent word for me to come?' Kajong replied: 'No!' The mother then realized that it was not Haloek but Kajong and she was ashamed before Kajong and went back home.

She had eaten almost all the salt meat when she found a hand bearing a ring, and recognized the hand and the ring of Haloek, her daughter. Then she knew her daughter was dead and that Kajong, possessed as she was of a supernatural power, had come back to life.

Benizara and Kakezara

Source: Keigo Seki, *Folktales of Japan*, London, Routledge & Kegan Paul, 1963. Translated by Robert J. Adams. Collected in Hamamatsu City, Shizuoka-ken, by Hana Watanabe.

This story is one of a number of related Japanese stepmother tales. Though neither Cox nor Rooth had access to them, there are numerous Japanese Cinderellas, traceable through the Japanese folktale indexes of Keigo Seki and Hiroko Ikeda. In 1964 Kenichi Mizusawa published in his *Echigo no Shinderera* (*Cinderella in Echigo*) no less than ninety-four Cinderella variants collected by him in a single district.

Robert Adams notes that Japanese bathtubs are deep and narrow, with a lid that makes them an ideal hiding place. Kakezara's poem is not only banal but technically incompetent, whereas Benizara's follows the 5–7–5–7–7 syllable arrangement of the *Waka* or *Tanka* poetic form.

'Benizara and Kakezara' may be compared with the 'Cinderella' in Eberhard's *Folktales of China*, in which the two sisters are called 'Beauty and Pockface'.

LONG AGO IN a certain place there were two sisters. One was named Benizara, 'Crimson Dish' and the other Kakezara, 'Broken Dish'. Benizara was a former wife's child, while Kakezara was the stepmother's child. Benizara was a very honest and gentle girl, but her stepmother was very cruel to her.

One day she sent the two girls out to gather chestnuts. She gave

Benizara a bag with a hole in the bottom, but she gave Kakezara a good one. 'You must not come back until you have each filled your bag,' she said.

The two set off for the mountains and began to pick up chestnuts. Before long Kakezara's bag was full, and she returned home, leaving Benizara alone. Benizara was an honest girl, and she worked as hard as she could picking up chestnuts until it began to get dark. It got darker and darker, and she thought she heard a rustling sound, *gasa gasa*, as though a wolf were coming toward her. She suddenly realized how dangerous it was and ran off without even looking where she was going. In the meantime it had become very dark and she was completely lost. She was filled with despair, but she knew that it would do no good to cry; so she kept on walking, thinking that perhaps she might find a house. Suddenly just ahead she saw a light. She went to where it was and found an old woman alone spinning thread. Benizara explained that she had gone to gather chestnuts but that it was late and she couldn't return home; then she asked if she might please stay overnight there.

The old woman said: 'I would like to let you stay here, but both my sons are *oni*. They will soon be coming home and would eat up anyone they found here. Instead, I will tell you how to find your way home.' And she carefully explained which road to take. Then she filled her bag with chestnuts and gave her a little box and a handful of rice. 'Take the chestnuts to your mother. This little box is a magic box; if there is ever anything that you need, just say what you would like, then tap on the box three times and what you want will appear. Now if you meet my *oni* sons on your way home, chew some of the rice and spread it around your mouth; then lie down and pretend that you are dead.'

Benizara thanked her for everything and started for home on the road she had been told to take. After a while she heard the sound of a flute coming toward her. She chewed some of the rice and spread it around her mouth, then lay down by the side of the road and pretended she was dead. Soon a red *oni* and a blue *oni* came along. 'Hey, older brother, I smell human beings,' said one and went over to the side of the road to look. 'It's no good, older brother, she's already rotten. Her mouth is full of worms,' he said. And they went on down the road blowing their flutes.

Benizara listened to the sound of the flutes growing fainter and fainter in the distance; then she continued on down the road that she had been told to take.

Soon morning came. At home her stepmother was thinking to herself that during the night the wolves would have surely eaten Benizara, when just then the girl arrived home. Far from being dead, she had a whole bag full of chestnuts; so the stepmother had nothing to scold her about.

One day some time after this a play was to be given in the village. The stepmother took Kakezara and went to see it, giving Benizara a great deal of work which had to be done before they returned home. Benizara was working as hard as she could, when some of her friends came and asked her to go with them to see the play. Benizara said that her stepmother had given her so much work to do that she could not go, but her friends said, 'We will help you and then you can go,' and so, all working together, they soon finished a whole day's work.

Her friends were all wearing beautiful kimonos, but Benizara had nothing but rags to wear. She wondered what she should do; then she thought about the little box she had received from the old woman in the mountains. She took it out and said that she would like to have a kimono. She was given a beautiful kimono. She put it on and went to see the play. When she got there, Kakezara was begging her mother for some candies and Benizara threw her some. When she did this, a nobleman who had come to see the performance of the play saw what happened.

The next day the nobleman's colorful procession came to the village. The lord's palanquin stopped in front of Benizara's house. Kakezara's mother was overjoyed and dressed Kakezara in her very best to meet him. The lord got out of the palanquin and said, 'There should be two girls here; bring out the other one too.'

The stepmother had put Benizara in the bath tub to hide her, but there was nothing she could do but obey the lord's command, and so she brought her out. In comparison to Kakezara, Benizara looked very shabby, but the lord said, 'Which one of these two came to see the performance of the play yesterday?'

'It was this one, Kakezara.'

'No, it wasn't that one,' said the lord, but the mother kept insisting that it was. Finally it was decided to ask each of them to compose a song. The lord took a plate and put it on a tray; then he piled some salt in the plate and stuck a pine needle in it. He commanded that they each compose a poem, using that as a subject.

In a loud voice Kakezara sang,

Benizara and Kakezara

Put a plate on a tray,
Put some salt on the plate,
Stick a pine needle in the salt;
It'll soon fall over.

Then she hit the lord on the head and ran off. Next Benizara sang,

A tray and plate, oh!
A mountain rises from the plate,
On it, snow has fallen.
Rooted deep into the snow,
A lonely pine tree grows.

When he heard this song, the lord praised it very highly. Preparations were soon made, and Benizara was put into a beautiful palanquin; then she rode off to the lord's palace.

Kakezara's mother watched in silence; then she put Kakezara in a huge empty basket, saying 'Now, Kakezara, you too may go to the lord's palace.' She dragged her along, but she did it so violently that Kakezara tumbled over the edge of a deep ditch and fell to her death.

Burenushka, the Little Red Cow

Source: Aleksandr Afanas'ev, *Russian Fairy Tales*, New York: Pantheon Books, 1945. Translated by Norbert Guterman.

The 'One-Eye, Two-Eyes and Three-Eyes' story is an elaboration of the very early oriental 'spying' motif. It is found predominantly in the Slavonic and Baltic regions, but also elsewhere: a recently recorded version by the Scottish traveller Betsy Whyte appears in Alan Bruford's excellent anthology *The Green Man of Knowledge*. This nineteenth-century Russian version concisely covers the main features of the story, familiar from the Grimms' 'One-Eye, Two-Eyes and Three-Eyes'. After the wedding, the story often develops into 'Little Brother and Little Sister' (AT450) or, as here, into the similar, 'The Black Bride and the White Bride' (AT403).

One thing which is not made clear in this version is quite how the little red cow supplies Princess Maria with her food and finery. One frequent device is for the girl to feed from the animal's ear, as in the Scottish/Australian 'Ashpitel', in which the black lamb tells Ashpitel 'to put her finger into its ear, and see what she could find'. She draws out bread and cheese, 'and had a good dinner, and felt quite happy'.

IN A CERTAIN KINGDOM, in a certain land, there lived a king and a queen, and they had an only daughter, Princess Maria. When the queen died, the king took another wife, Yagishna. Yagishna gave birth to two daughters: one had two eyes, and the other three eyes. The stepmother disliked Princess Maria, and ordered her to take Burenushka, the little red cow, to pasture, and gave her a crust of dry bread for her dinner. The princess went to the open field, bowed to Burenushka's right leg, ate and drank her fill, and dressed in fine attire; all day long, dressed like a lady, she tended Burenushka. At the end of the day, she again bowed to the little cow's right leg, removed her fine attire, went home carrying back her crust of bread, and put it on the table. 'How does the slut keep alive?' wondered Yagishna. The next day she gave Princess Maria the same crust, and sent her elder daughter with her, saying, 'Give an eye to what Princess Maria feeds herself with.' They came to the open field and Princess Maria said: 'Little sister, let me pick the lice from your head.' She began to pick them, at the same time saying: 'Sleep, sleep, little sister! Sleep, sleep, my dear! Sleep, sleep, little eye! Sleep, sleep, other eye!' The sister fell asleep, and Princess Maria rose up, went to Burenushka, bowed to her right leg, ate and drank her fill, dressed herself in fine attire, and all day long walked around like a lady. Night came; Princess Maria removed her fine attire and said: 'Get up, little sister, get up, my dear, let us go home.' 'Ah,' said the sister unhappily, 'I have slept through the day, and have not seen anything; now my mother will scold me.' They came home; the mother asked her: 'What did Princess Maria eat, what did she drink?' 'I have not seen anything.' Yagishna scolded her; next morning she got up and sent her three-eyed daughter, saying: 'Go and see what that slut eats and drinks.' The girls came to the open field where Burenushka grazed, and Princess Maria said: 'Little sister, let me pick the lice from your head.' 'Pick them, little sister! Pick them, my dear!' Princess Maria began to pick, saying at the same time: 'Sleep, sleep, little sister! Sleep, sleep, my dear! Sleep, sleep, little eye! Sleep, sleep, other eye!' She forgot about the third eye, and the third eye looked and looked at what Princess Maria was doing. She ran to Burenushka, bowed to her right leg, ate and drank her fill, dressed in fine attire. When the sun began to set, she again bowed to Burenushka, removed her fine attire, and went to rouse the three-eyed one: 'Get up, little sister! Get up, my dear! Let us go home!' Princess Maria came home and put her dry crusts on the table. The mother questioned her daughter. 'What does she eat and drink?' The three-eyed one told everything. Yagishna said to her husband: 'Slaughter Burenushka, old man!' And the old man slaughtered the cow. Princess Maria begged him: 'Please, my dear, give me at least a bit of the entrails!' The old man threw her a bit of the entrails. She took it, placed it on a gatepost, and a bush with sweet berries grew up on it, and all kinds of little birds perched there and sang songs of kings and of peasants. Prince Ivan heard about Princess Maria, came to her stepmother, put a dish on the table and said: 'Whichever maiden picks a dishful of berries for me, her I will take as my wife.' Yagishna sent her elder daughter to pick berries; the birds did not even let her come near, she had to guard her eyes lest the birds peck them out. Yagishna sent her other daughter, and they did not let her come close either. At last she sent Princess Maria. Princess Maria took the dish and went to pick the berries; and as she picked them, the little birds placed twice and thrice as many on the dish as she herself could pick. She returned, placed the berries on the table, and bowed to the prince. There was a gay feast and a wedding; Prince Ivan took Princess Maria away, and they began to live happily and prospered.

After some time, a long time or a short time, Princess Maria gave birth to a son. She wanted to visit her father, and went to his house with her husband. Her stepmother turned her into a goose and disguised her elder daughter as Prince Ivan's wife. Prince Ivan returned home. The old tutor of the child got up early in the morning, washed himself very clean, took the baby in his arms and went to an open field, stopping near a little bush. Geese came flying, gray geese came. 'My geese, gray geese! Where have you seen the baby's mother?' 'In the next flock.' The next flock came. 'My geese, gray geese! Where have you seen the baby's mother?' The baby's mother jumped to the ground, tore off her goose skin, took the baby in her arms, and nursed him at her breast, crying: 'I will nurse him today, I will nurse him tomorrow, but the day after I will fly beyond the forest dark, beyond the mountains high!' The old man went home. The little fellow slept till next morning without awakening, and the false wife railed at the old man for having gone to the open field and for having starved her son. Next morning again he got up very early, washed himself very clean, and went with the child to the open field; and Prince Ivan got up, followed the old man unseen, and hid in the bush. Geese came flying, gray geese came. The old man called to them: 'My geese, gray geese! Where have you seen the baby's mother?' 'In the next flock.' The next flock came. 'My geese, gray geese! Where have you seen the baby's mother?' The baby's mother jumped to the ground, tore off her goose skin, threw it behind the bush, nursed the baby at her breast, and said farewell to him: 'Tomorrow I will fly beyond the forests dark, beyond the mountains high!' She gave the baby to the old man and said: 'Why is there a smell of burning?' She turned to put her goose skin on, and realized that it was gone: Prince Ivan had burned it. He grasped Princess Maria; she turned into a frog, then into a lizard, and into one kind of loathsome insect after another, and at last into a spindle. Prince Ivan broke the spindle in two, threw the top back of him and the bottom in front of him, and a beautiful young woman stood before him. They went home together. Yagishna's daughter yelled and shouted: 'The wrecker is

coming, the killer is coming!' Prince Ivan gathered the dukes and boyars together and asked them: 'With which wife do you advise me to live?' They said: 'With the first.' 'Well, gentlemen, whichever wife is the first to climb the gate, with her I will live.' Yagishna's daughter at once climbed to the top of the gate, but Princess Maria only clutched it and did not climb. Then Prince Ivan took his gun and shot the false wife, and began to live with Princess Maria as of old, and they prospered.

The Poor Girl and her Cow

Source: E. S. Stevens, *Folk-Tales of 'Iraq, set down and translated from the vernacular*, London, Oxford University Press, 1931.

This story was narrated to Ethel Stefana Stevens (afterwards Lady Drower) by Lili, an illiterate Baghdad Christian woman. There is a photograph of her as a frontispiece to the book, for which she was a major source. Stevens does not, however, give much further information about her.

Stevens characterizes this as 'among the most-told folk-tales of the Middle and Near East'. She notes particularly Persian and Armenian variants, and European parallels. A very similar story can be found in M. Wardrop, *Georgian Folk Tales*.

With regard to this tale, E. S. Stevens explains that the *šilūwa* is an 'Iraqi water-spirit, shaped like a woman but with long pendulous breasts and sometimes a fish's tail. The *šilūwa* is partial to both human flesh and human lovers. *Kalabdūn*, to which the girl's hair is compared, is the gold wire used in embroidering the garments known as *'abas*, especially round the neck and at the edges.

Oral narrators are generally more interested in following the shape of the story than in condensing for speed and concision. Frequently adventures are first described by the narrator and then retold at equal length inside the story. Such was apparently the case here, when the stepmother asks the girl how her hair comes to be golden.

THERE WAS ONCE a couple who had an only child, a daughter, of whom they were very fond. In time the mother died, leaving her cow to her daughter, and the father married again, his second wife bringing him another daughter. The two girls grew up together, but the step-mother did not love the first wife's child and made her life very difficult.

Now the orphaned girl discovered that the cow which her mother had left her had a wonderful gift. If she gave it cotton to eat, it returned it all spun. This she took to the Sūq al Ghazl, the Market of the Spinners, and sold it. Each day the girl took the cow into the desert, and there the cow spun her cotton.

The step-mother was angered with the girl for her absences, and said to her husband, 'That girl takes her cow every day and goes off into the desert. You must kill the cow!'

Answered the father, '*Khatiya!* That would be a sin! The girl has done nothing evil, and the cow was left to her by her mother. What good would it do if I were to kill it?' And he refused.

One day, when the girl was in the desert, two pieces of the cotton which the cow was spinning for her flew away on the wind, and the girl ran after them till they reached a cave, before which there ran a water-channel, and in this cave was a śilūwa milling flour between two stones, her teats thrown backwards over her shoulder, after the fashion of the śilūwat.

The girl picked up some of the flour which had fallen out, and sucked some of the śilūwa's milk.

The śilūwa turned round and said:

'Had I seen you before you had drunk of my milk and eaten of my flour, I should have made one mouthful of you, but as it is, you are my daughter. Now, I wish to sleep at the mouth of the cave. I will put my head on your lap, and you can take the lice from my head, and all that you catch, bite them up!'

The girl looked this way and that, and she spied some loose grains of corn lying about, and she picked up a handful of them.

Then the śilūwa reclined, and put her head on the girl's lap, and said,

> *If the water runs white, rouse me,*
> *If it runs yellow, rouse me,*
> *But if it runs black, do not rouse me.*

Answered the girl, 'As you order, my mother, sleep!'

And the śilūwa slept, and the girl began to pluck the lice out of her head, and what a lot of horrid creatures they were! Black, white, large, small! From time to time the girl put the wheat into her mouth and said, 'How sweet your lice are, my mother! I am enjoying them.'

Presently, she saw that the water in the channel ran white, and she roused the śilūwa saying, 'The water is white!' Said the śilūwa, 'Rise, go and wash in the water.'

The girl did as the śilūwa told her, and when she came out of the water, *subhān Allah!* she was as fair as the morning! The girl returned, and the śilūwa slept again with her head on her lap, while the girl picked the lice from her head. Presently the channel ran yellow, and she roused the śilūwa and told her, 'The water runs yellow!'

The śilūwa said, 'Rise, go and dip your head in it.'

The girl dipped her head in the water, as she was bid, and when she lifted her head and shook the water from it, her hair was yellow as kalabdūn, glittering like gold, and so long that it reached her knees.

But when the girl saw it, she was afraid, and said to the śilūwa, 'Alas, why have you done this to me? When she sees me, my step-mother will ask me what I have been doing and will perhaps be angry with me.'

Said the śilūwa, 'Tie your head in a rag and go back. Do not fear! Your step-mother will kill your cow.'

When she heard that, the girl began to cry.

And the śilūwa said, 'Do not eat of its flesh, but put the bones and skin and all that remains of the cow into a bag, and go to the place where she spins cloth from the cotton, and bury the bag there and leave it there for forty days. At the end of that time, take it out, and whatever you find in the bag is yours.'

So the girl left the cave and returned to her cow and drove it back to her father's house. When she saw her, the step-mother began to abuse her and revile her, saying, 'Where have you been? Why have you dallied so long? You bring shame on us. I shall tell your father, and ask him to kill your cow.'

The girl began to weep, but the step-mother went to the father and said, 'Your daughter is always gadding and gives the excuse of her cow. So now you must slaughter it.'

The father said, '*Khatiya!* That would be a sin! My daughter loves her cow, and it was the gift of her mother who is dead.'

Said the step-mother, 'Either you kill it, or I leave the house.'

So the father rose, and went to the cow and slaughtered it, and skinned it, and cleaned it, and threw the head and the skin and hoofs and entrails away. Then the step-mother cooked the meat, but the girl refused to eat it.

They said to her, 'Eat, eat! The flesh is good.'

She said, 'Never! I will not eat of the cow!'

And she went secretly, and put the skin and bones and head and tail and feet and entrails into a bag, and took it out into the desert, and buried it in the place where her cow used to graze and spin her cotton. Then she returned to the house, and every day she wept about the cow.

One day she wished to comb her hair, so she went on the roof, and took off the rag about her head and combed it.

The step-mother came out to see what she was doing on the roof, and the girl's hair was streaming out like the rays of the sun, and shining like gold.

Said the step-mother, 'How did you get your hair like that?'

Answered the girl, 'It was the śilūwa,' and she told her how she had followed the two pieces of cotton to the śilūwa's cave, and all that had happened to her there.

The step-mother said, 'Go, return to the cave, and take my daughter with you to the śilūwa, and ask her to make my girl's hair like yours.'

So the girl went with her step-sister, and on the road she told her all that had happened, so that the girl might know what to do.

The other girl was stupid, and she said, 'I cannot remember all this!'

When they came to the cave, the second girl did as her sister had told her, and ate of the flour on the ground, and sucked the śilūwa's milk from the dugs that hung over her shoulder.

Then the śilūwa turned and said to her, 'Child of Adam, if you had not drunk of my milk and eaten of my flour, and become my daughter, I should have made one mouthful of you.'

Then she said as she had said to the first girl, 'Sit by the mouth of the cave, and I will put my head in your lap so that you may pick out the lice while I am asleep.'

The girl sat down, and the śilūwa put her head in her lap, and the girl began to pick out the lice. But when she saw what was in the śilūwa's hair, she began to scream, and said, 'What creatures! I am afraid.'

Then the śilūwa said,

If the channel runs black do not rouse me,

43

> *If the channel runs yellow, rouse me,*
> *If the channel runs white, rouse me.*

Then she went to sleep. Presently, the girl, who had not listened well to what she said, roused her, saying, 'The channel has run black.'

The šilūwa answered, 'Rise, go and wash your head in it.'

The girl rose, and went and plunged her head into the water. And when she withdrew it, there were two black horns on her head!

The šilūwa said, 'Did I not tell you "do not rouse me if the water is black".'

And she sent the girl away, and the two sisters returned weeping, and the younger uglier than before.

When the step-mother saw her daughter, she was very angry and asked what had happened. Said the first girl, 'It was not my fault, I told her what to do.'

Said the second, 'She told me, but I forgot.'

The step-mother was angrier than ever, and said to her own daughter, 'You owl! Why did you not listen!'

Now the elder girl was counting the days, and *dī dī dī!* they passed, until it was the fortieth. Then she went into the desert and dug in the place where she had buried the bag.

When she had uncovered it and opened it, what did she see! The skin had become an 'āba all embroidered with gold, the tail had become a dress of silk, and the bones and the rest were changed into jewellery, each bone a piece; chains of pearls, bracelets, and precious stones, and amongst the rest were a pair of clogs set with diamonds and emeralds. Never was there such an outfit in all the world!

The girl was so delighted that she put on her finery and admired herself in the brook, and when she had pleasured herself enough, she took them off, and put them in the bag, and buried them again. Then she returned to her house in her old clothes.

Every day she returned to the place, and put on her finery and looked at herself in the brook, and then took it off and returned home.

One day when she was so arrayed and adorned, there came by the son of the Sultan, whose house was near that place, and he watched her. When she had finished adorning herself, she changed her clothes, and folded up her 'āba and jewellery, and hid them in the sack and buried them. But as she was hiding them she saw that some one was looking, and in her haste she forgot one clog, which slipped into the brook.

When she had gone, the Sultan's son called a servant, and said, 'In the brook there is a clog, go into the water and get it.'

The servant went into the brook and searched for it, and found it. He wrapped it up and brought it to the Sultan's son.

When the Sultan's son saw it, he exclaimed, 'What a clog! Such a fine one I have never seen.' Then he went to his mother and said to her, 'My mother, I wish to marry the owner of this clog.'

His mother answered, 'Good, my son.'

She took a slave, and she went into the town and she tried at one house after another, but the clog fitted no girl: for one it was too long, for another too short, for another too broad, and for another too narrow. At last she came to the house where the two sisters lived; it was the last house.

When she knew that the Sultan's wife had come to find a bride for her son, the step-mother took her step-daughter, and put her in the oven, and shut the cover down on her; but her own daughter she adorned, and dressed in fine clothes.

When the Sultan's wife saw her, she said, 'Is this your only daughter?'

The woman answered, 'Aye, I have no other, this is the only girl.'

And the girl in the oven cried out, 'Oh, oh, oh, Fatma Khān! My feet stick out of the hole.'

The step-mother cried angrily, 'Hush! Hush!'

The Sultan's wife said, 'Who is that? Let her speak.'

The girl cried out again, 'Oh, oh, oh! Fatma Khān, my feet are sticking out.'

Said the Sultan's wife, 'I think there is a girl in the oven.'

Said the step-mother, 'No – that is a cat.'

Said the Sultan's wife, 'No, but I hear her,' and she went to the oven, and there were the girl's feet sticking out. So she opened the oven and bade her come out.

Said the Sultan's wife, 'Put the clog on the foot of this one.'

And the girl put the clog on her foot, and it fitted perfectly, as a ring fits a finger.

Then the Sultan's wife said, 'I will take this one for my son.'

And they called the mulla and made the betrothal and there was a marriage for seven days and for seven nights.

An Armenian Cinderella

Source: Susie Hoogasian-Villa, *100 Armenian Tales and Their Folkloristic Relevance*, Detroit, Wayne State University Press, 1966. Narrated by Mrs Mariam Serabian.

The following story was collected in Detroit in 1940–42, as part of extensive field-work among the Detroit Armenian community by Susie Hoogasian-Villa. It was told by Mrs Mariam Serabian, the collector's grandmother, who was then in her seventies, having emigrated to America in 1923.

Popular traditions of all kinds can be kept surprisingly vital in a transplanted setting by a close-knit immigrant community. No tradition is ever static, and there are of course developments and changes, but it is possible to argue that such communities are in some ways more conservative, because the traditions are both a link with and an expression of the homeland.

Susie Hoogasian-Villa notes four Armenian variants. None of these, however, has the cannibalistic opening which is this narration's most interesting feature. This motif seems to be confined to the Near East and the Balkans. Cox has four examples (17, 50, 53 and 124), two from Greece, one from Cyprus and one from Dalmatia. Cox 50, from Epirus, was translated by the Rev. E. M. Geldart as 'Little Saddleslut'. It opens:

> There were once three sisters spinning flax, and they said, 'Whoever spindle falls, let us kill her and eat her.'
>
> The mother's spindle fell, and they left her alone.
>
> Again they sat down to spin, and again the mother's spindle fell, and again and yet again. 'Ah, well!' said they, 'let us eat her now!'

'No!' said the youngest, 'do not eat her; eat me, if flesh you will have.'

But they would not; and two of them killed their mother and cooked her for eating.

When they had sat down to make a meal of her, they said to the youngest, 'Come and eat too!'

But she refused, and sat down on a saddle which the fowls were covering with filth, and wept, and upbraided them.

AT ONE TIME there lived an old couple who had three daughters. When the father died, he left them a little money, but, as we all know, money which is not added to but always taken from will soon disappear. So it was now, and the sisters and their mother were soon left penniless.

The two elder sisters continually reminded their mother that they were poor and had nothing to eat, but the youngest sister never complained.

'Let us go out and get food, no matter what we must do,' the elder sisters said.

'No, don't do that,' the mother said, 'I would prefer that you kill me and eat me rather than bring dishonor to this home.'

'No! No! I will never let them do that!' the youngest sister said, crying.

For ten days the two sisters told their mother that they were hungry, and for ten days the mother gave them the same answer. So on the tenth day the sisters decided to kill their mother.

'Oh! Mother, I will not let them do this!' the youngest daughter cried and threw herself on her mother's neck.

When the older girls were away, the mother took her youngest child aside and said, 'Don't cry, my child. They will kill me, I know this: nothing can be done. Let them eat as much as they want, but don't you eat. After they have finished, take my bones and bury them behind the house. Whenever you need anything – whether it be food, clothes, money – just come to my grave and ask for it, and it shall be yours. When you no longer need it, dig the ground a little and stick it in. But don't ever let your sisters know this,' the mother said.

And so it happened. The cruel sisters killed their mother and sat down to eat her. 'Come, eat!' the two sisters urged, but the youngest girl refused, saying, 'I will not eat my mother's flesh.' The older sisters did not worry at all since now they had all the more to eat.

When the two sisters had finished and left the house, the youngest sister took her mother's bones and buried them behind the house. Meanwhile, in the days following, the youngest girl reminded her sisters over and over that they had killed their mother and eaten her.

One day the king announced to all his people, rich and poor alike, that his one and only son was to be married, and everyone was invited to the wedding feast. The two sisters were much excited, and when they were both dressed in their best finery, they asked their youngest sister why she was not ready.

'Why should I go with you? You killed my mother and ate her,' she said, crying. They gave her a blow on the head and left.

When the sisters were gone, the youngest sister went to her mother's grave where she asked for a beautiful blue dress. Immediately on the ground before her appeared a lovely blue gown. The young girl combed her hair and put on the lovely dress. Such beauty as hers was not for human eyes! At the feast everyone noticed the beautiful girl, but no one could learn her name. When the youngest sister saw that it was getting late, she slipped out unnoticed and returned home. She changed her clothes and hid the dress as she had been told to do.

When the sisters returned, they said, 'You should have been there today! There was such a beautiful girl, but no one knew who she was!'

'Why should I go with you? You killed my mother and ate her,' the youngest said.

The two sisters, angered by this reminder, gave her another blow and went to bed. The next evening the two again prepared to go to the wedding feast and asked their youngest sister to go with them.

'Why should I go with you? You killed my mother and ate her,' the youngest sister said. Again the sisters hit her and started on their way. The youngest sister went behind the house and asked for a second dress. When it appeared, she washed, combed her hair, put on her dress and started for the palace.

Again everyone marveled at her beauty and wondered who she was. The king, too, became curious and ordered his men to follow her.

But on the second evening, as on the first, the youngest sister slipped out of the palace without being discovered. She hurriedly went home, changed, hid her dress and was ready for her sisters' return.

'Oh! You should have come with us tonight! The beautiful girl was there again! She sparkled like a jewel!' the two sisters said.

'Why should I go with you? You killed my mother and ate her,' the youngest sister said. Again the sisters grew angry, beat their youngest sister and went to bed.

The third day of the wedding the two sisters put on their best dresses and asked their youngest sister if she would go with them.

'No, why should I go with you? You killed my mother and ate her,' the youngest sister answered. The cruel sisters hit her again and left.

When the youngest sister found herself alone, she went behind the house and asked her mother for a third dress. When it appeared, she washed, combed her hair, put on the dress and went to the palace. Now the king had heard such descriptions of the beautiful creature who came to the ball every night that he decided to see for himself how true this talk was. He hid himself so that he could see the people without being seen. How true! She was as lovely as they had said and even lovelier! Who was she? He called some of his men together and ordered them not to let her pass out of their sight for even one moment. The youngest sister saw that she was surrounded with men all that evening but did not know why. Again she slipped out of the palace without being noticed. The king was furious and told his men that they would be punished if they did not catch her the next night.

The youngest sister went home, changed her clothes, concealed her dress and sat down to wait for her sisters. When they returned, they spoke of the beautiful girl and asked their youngest sister why she did not go with them.

'Why should I go with you? You killed my mother and ate her,' the youngest sister said, whereupon the two older sisters beat her and went to bed.

The fourth day the two sisters again made ready for the wedding feast. Again they asked their youngest sister to go with them. 'Why should I go with you? You killed and ate my mother,' the youngest said. The two sisters beat her once more and left for the wedding. When the girl was alone, she went behind the house to her mother's grave and asked for a beautiful dress. She washed, combed her hair, put on the dress and started out.

The king, not wishing to take a chance of losing her, disguised himself and with his men surrounded her constantly. When she saw that it was getting late, she slipped out of the palace, but this time she did not go unnoticed. The king and several of his men followed her and saw her enter a house. They knocked on the door and said to her, 'What are you doing here? Come, the king wants to see you.'

'This is where I live, why else would I be here?' the girl answered. 'What does the king want with me?'

'Aren't you proud that the king wants to see you?' they asked.

'I can't go to the king now; I have two sisters who are at the wedding.'

'Well, let them stay behind,' the guards said.

'No, they killed my mother and ate her,' the girl said, beginning to cry.

'What is this?' the men asked in surprise.

So the youngest sister told them the story of her mother's death. 'When my mother knew that my sisters were going to kill her, she told me to save her bones and bury them in the back of the house. She told me whenever I needed anything – money, food, dresses – to go to her grave and ask for it, and I would receive it. And after I had finished using it, I was to bury it in the ground,' the girl said.

'What! Is such a thing possible?' the king (who was in disguise among his men) asked. 'Show me how you do this.'

The youngest sister took the men behind the house. She asked for a dress, and a dress appeared through the ground. The king told his men to dig into the ground and see what else was beneath it. The men found dishes, clothes, slippers and everything a girl would want. The king was astonished.

While they were puzzling over this, the two older sisters returned home. 'All you do is sit home and cry all the time. You should have been with us to see the beautiful girl today. Now you will never see her because today was the last day of the wedding,' the sisters said.

'Why should I go with you? You killed and ate my mother,' she answered. The two older sisters gave her a good beating and then went to bed.

The next morning a troop of soldiers came to the door and took the two elder girls before the king. 'Since you killed your mother, you are to be put in prison,' he ruled. The two sisters tried in every way they knew to deny this deed, but, of course, they could not change matters. So they were put in prison.

The same day the king went to the girl's house and carried off the youngest sister. They celebrated a big wedding for forty days and forty nights. Meanwhile, the two sisters, who were in prison, did not know what had happened to their youngest sister.

One day the king told his wife, 'I will build a church where your mother's home stood and have a beautiful statue placed where her bones are buried.' So a beautiful church was built, and a tall statue with the mother's name written on it was set over the mother's grave. 'Now you can go every morning to this church and pray,' the king told his wife, hoping that this would ease her sorrow.

However, the king was still angry about the cruel deed of the sisters and wanted them killed. But the youngest sister pleaded and finally convinced him to free them instead. Because the king loved his wife dearly, he set the two sisters free. They returned home to find that their house did not exist, but in its place there now stood a beautiful church. Near it they saw a large statue of their mother. They were much surprised, because, of course, they didn't know that their youngest sister had brought this about. They asked their neighbors about this but no one would tell them what had happened.

One morning when the youngest sister was leaving this church, she saw her two sisters walking in the churchyard. She ran and fell at their feet. The two sisters were much surprised. Who were they that such a noble lady should fall at their feet?

'Don't you recognize me, sisters?' the queen said.

When the two heard this rich and beautifully dressed lady call them 'sisters', they looked again and recognized their youngest sister. The two older sisters started crying, and the youngest joined them. After a while they forgave one another. The two sisters left the town, and the youngest sister went back to the palace. When she reached home, she told the king about her meeting, and he was happy that the sisters had forgiven one another.

The king and queen lived happily ever after.

Askenbasken, who Became Queen

Source: Evald Tang Kristensen, *Jyske Folkeminder* V, Copenhagen, 1881. Told by Mads Krist. Madsen, Fastrup, Jutland. Translated by Joan Rockwell.

The galoshes are a homely touch in this particularly concentrated and powerful Cinderella. The conclusion echoes that of the Grimms' 'Aschenputtle'; it is possible there has been some influence. The savage ending was added only in the second edition of Grimm, reflecting the Grimms' fondness for violent moral retribution.

Kristensen collected a great many Cinderella variants. Joan Rockwell, author of his biography, *Evald Tang Kristensen: A Lifelong Adventure in Folklore*, estimates around fifty, scattered amongst his voluminous published and unpublished collections. Cox abstracts twelve of these.

THERE WAS A WOMAN who had three daughters, only one of them was a stepdaughter. This girl she treated very ill: she was never allowed to go out with the others on visits, and was always kept at home where she slept in a corner of the kitchen among all the dirt and ashes, and so she was called Askenbasken.

The other two daughters, though, were always dressed up very fine, so that they looked like real young ladies.

There was to be a great ball in the neighbourhood, and the father was to go to the market town and buy fine clothes for the two elder sisters. He asked them what they would have, and they demanded one elegant thing and bit of finery after another. But when he asked Askenbasken what she would have, she said she only wanted a rose-tree, with the roots and all. She wanted to plant it on her mother's grave, but she dare not say so, and her father wondered a good deal why she made this wish, but he bought the rose-tree just the same.

That night when all was still, she stole out of the house and took the tree to her mother's grave where she planted it, and watered it with her tears.

From now on she went there every evening, to see her rose-tree, and it grew so well and was so beautiful that it was a joy to see. But she was even more delighted when she noticed that a white dove came and sat singing in the tree whenever she came; and it sang so sweetly she had never heard anything so rare.

In the meantime the two sisters were getting their finery ready to go to the ball, and they spent all their time arranging it. Askenbasken would also have liked to go, and she asked if she might. The stepmother didn't quite like to say straight out that she couldn't go, so she flung a plateful of peas into the ashes, and said, If she could gather them up again, each and every one, she could come along to the ball, and they'd find some old rags or other to hang on her.

Anyone would have thought this was an impossible task, and that's what the stepmother thought too. But just as Askenbasken was kneeling and groping for the peas in the ashes, the white dove came flying right against the windowpane under the roof. She went out and let the dove in, and it had a whole troop of birds with it. They all set to work to peck and pick up all the peas, and so they were all collected in a twinkling. But when the girl showed them to her mother, she was so furious that she took a whole apron-full of peas and threw them in the ashes, saying that now Askenbasken could just gather up all those before she came to the ball. Since the ball was to begin that very same afternoon, she was pretty sure not to have Askenbasken dragging along with them.

Soon after this the others drove off, and Askenbasken went up to her mother's grave and cried bitterly. But then the white dove came, and sang that she should cheer up and go home, and there she would find a grand dress she could put on and go to the ball, but she must be sure to get home before the others.

So she got to the ball, and there was no one there more elegant or better dressed than she, and besides that she was a very handsome girl herself. The king himself was there, and he was so pleased with this fair stranger that he danced with her the whole evening. The mother was so insulted because he didn't dance at all with her daughters that she decided to go home far earlier than she had intended. When Askenbasken noticed this, she hurried away from the ball herself and had her fine clothes hidden away before the others got home.

When they did get home, Askenbasken was sly enough to ask them how they had enjoyed the ball. 'What's that to do with you, you scarecrow?' they answered; and that was all the reply she got.

The next day they were to go to the ball again. The girls were dressed much finer even than the day before, and off they drove and left Askenbasken to her own devices at home. Away she went to her mother's grave and cried, and immediately the dove came and sat in the rose-tree and sang of the fine clothes that lay at home waiting for her to put them on; but she must be sure to be the first one home.

That evening the king sat with his eyes fixed on the door, for he longed to see the lovely girl from the day before, and had promised himself that she would not slip away from him so easily a second time. In she came, and the king was so much in love that he danced with no one else. But the mother was so envious because her own daughters never got a dance, even though they were decked out so splendidly, that she decided to go home at once, and wouldn't stay a moment longer at any price. Now Askenbasken too had to hurry away, and she really had to shove the king aside, for he tried to hold her.

But she did get home in time, and hid her fine clothes.

'Well, did you have a good time?' she asked when the others came home. 'Mind your own business, Ash-poker,' said they.

There was to be a ball again on the third day, which was to be the last day of the festivities. The girls were going to try their luck one more time, so they dressed themselves up and tricked themselves out as fine as ever they could. But the king's eyes were fixed to the door the whole time, waiting for the mysterious beauty, and he had promised himself that he really would hold on to her this evening. When the others had left, Askenbasken went up her mother's grave and wept, and the dove came and sang that the clothes were lying at home and she should go to the ball, but be sure to come home before the others.

And so she went to the ball, and on this evening her clothes were like the purest gold, and she also had golden shoes on, and galoshes to wear as she walked the road, to keep them from getting muddy. Everything went as before, the old woman was insulted and wanted to go home. The king did his best, but the girl tricked him and ran away and though he ran after her he caught nothing but one of her shoes which stuck on the steps as she ran down and flew off her foot.

When the others got home, the clothes were hidden and there she sat in her corner of the kitchen as usual.

'Well, did you a have a good time?'

'None of your business, you slipshod wench,' said they, and that was all the answer she got.

But now the king had the shoe, and he resolved to ride around the country with it, until he found the girl that it would fit. He travelled here and he travelled there, but there was no one who could wear his shoe. At last he came to the house where they all lived, and he asked the woman if she had any daughters. Yes, she had two. In that case they must try the shoe.

But the eldest could not get it on, for her great toe was too long. Her old mother whispered in her ear, 'Cut it off! Better to lose a toe than lose a chance of being queen!' So she went in and took a great knife from the table and cut off her toe. Now she could get the shoe on, and so she was to go home with the king. He rode off with her accordingly, but as they passed the churchyard there sat the dove in the rose-tree and sang:

> *King, just look at the foot of the bride!*
> *Blood is running down inside!*

So he took a look at the shoe, and sure enough, blood was pouring out of it. When he saw that, he rode back and returned the girl, she certainly was not the one he wanted, and he didn't want to be swindled again; but didn't they have another daughter?

Yes, they did have another; and so she was to try on the shoe.

But with her the heel was too thick, and she couldn't push her foot all the way down.

'That's no great problem,' whispered her mother in her ear. 'You can always slice a bit off a heel, and it's far better to lose part of a heel than to lose the chance of being queen.' So she too went in and took the knife, and sliced a layer off her heel. Now she could get the shoe on, and so she was to go home with the king. But as she rode past the churchyard by his side, the dove sat again in the tree and sang:

> *King, just look at the foot of the bride,*
> *Blood is running down inside!*

And when he looked, sure enough the blood was pouring down, just as the bird sang. So what he did was to ride straight back and say, Now they had fooled him twice, and he had no mind to be swindled again. But didn't they have another daughter? Well, they did as a matter of fact have a sort of simple one, but there was no question of it being her, for she hadn't even been to the ball.

'Let's see her anyway,' said the king, 'it's just barely possible the shoe might fit her.'

So the mother called her and in she came, dirty and sooty and covered with ash, she looked a perfect mess.

'You could at least have brushed the ashes off,' said the old woman. 'It doesn't matter,' said the king. 'No one should be ashamed of the work they do. Do you think you could wear this shoe, little girl?'

'Of course I can,' said she, 'for it is my own.'

'Where did you get it?' says the mother in a rage.

'I see how it is,' said the king, 'of course she has some fine clothes laid away, like other folk. Go in, my girl, and put on the dress you wore on the first evening of the ball.'

So she did, and when she came back the king said, 'Now I have found the one I was looking for, and now you must come with me.'

And with that he took her up on his own horse with him, and rode away with her. When they passed the churchyard the dove sang:

See them riding in all their pride,
Now he has found his rightful bride.

And now they were to be married, it was a settled thing, and great preparations were made for the wedding. Her sisters were to be the bridesmaids since they were her closest kin, and so they were invited. But as they walked into the church the dove flew down and pecked the left eye out of each of them, and so they were blind in one eye. Then when they walked out of the church it flew down again and plucked the right eye out of each of them, so they were blind in both eyes. This was their punishment for being so cruel to their sister.

And ever after the king lived happily with the girl who had been called Askenbasken, but now had to be called queen; for now she was in her rightful place.

Ashey Pelt

Source: M. Damant, 'Folk Tales', *Folk-Lore* 6, London, The Folk-Lore Society, 1895.

Damant writes, 'The following tale was told me by a woman now living, a native of Ulster, aged about 60.' It is perhaps the brevity of this tale that allows the voice to lift off the page with such individual vitality.

The idea that the mother is actually a ewe is – as in the Inverness-shire story given in the notes to Cox – the result of narrative degeneration rather than the survival of archaic traits. It is very rare for Cinderella stories to depict the helpful animal as the physical mother. In 'The Wicked Stepmother' in J. H. Knowles's *Folk-Tales of Kashmir*, the real mother is turned into a goat.

WELL, MY GRANDMOTHER she told me that in them auld days a ewe might be your mother. It is a very lucky thing to have a black ewe. A man married again, and his daughter, Ashey Pelt, was unhappy. She cried alone, and the black ewe came to her from under the greystone in the field and said, 'Don't cry, go and find a rod behind the stone and strike it three times, and whatever you want will come.' So she did as she was bid. She wanted to go to a party. Dress and horses and all came to her, but she was bound to be back before twelve o'clock or all the enchantment would go, all she had would vanish. The sisters they did na' like her, she was so pretty, and the step-mother she kept her in wretchedness just.

She was most lovely. At the party the Prince fell in love with her, and she forgot to get back in time. In her speed a-running she dropped her *silk* slipper, and he sent and he went over all the country to find the lady it wad fit. When he came to Ashey Pelt's door he did not see her. The sisters was busy a-nipping and a-clipping at their feet to get on the silk slipper, for the king's son he had given out that he loved that lady sae weel he wad be married on whaever could fit on that slipper.

The sisters they drove Ashey Pelt out bye to be out of the road, and they bid her mind the cows. They pared down their feet till one o'them could just squeeze it on. But she was in the quare agony I'm telling you.

So off they rode away; but when he was passing the field the voice of the auld ewe cried on him to stop, and she says, says she –

> *Nippet foot, and clippet foot*
> *Behind the king's son rides,*
> *But bonny foot, and pretty foot*
> *Is with the cathering hides.*

So he rode back and found her among the cows, and he married her, and if they lived happy, so may you and me.

Rashin Coatie

Source: Andrew Lang, 'Rashin Coatie. A Scotch Tale'. *Revue Celtique* 3, Paris: 1876–8. Told by Miss Margaret Craig, Darliston, Elgin.

This Morayshire story is unusual in that the heroine is persecuted by her stepmother and not, as in most 'Cap o' Rushes' tales, by her father. The story of 'Rashie-Coat' in R. Chambers's *Popular Rhymes of Scotland* (1826) is a lightly disguised 'unnatural father' story ('her father wanted her to be married; but she didna like the man'), with very similar rhymes. 'The Red Calf' (W. Gregor, 'Three folk-tales from Old Meldrum', *Folk-Lore Journal* 2, 1884) is a similar story, with elements of the male Cinderella pattern of 'The Little Red Ox' (see 'The Bracket Bull' p. 95). The heroine of 'The Red Calf' is also called Rashin-Coatie, and again the rhymes are very similar to the text below. 'Mary Rashie-coats an the Wee Black Bull', a fine long story of Duncan Williamson's recorded by Linda Williamson in 1985 and published in their collection *A Thorn in the King's Foot*, also adapts 'The Little Red Ox' to a heroine, though it includes elements of various tale types. A rashin coatie is a garment made from reed fibres.

THERE WAS A KING and a Queen, as mony anes been, few have we seen, and as few may we see. The Queen, she deeit, and left a bonny little lassie; and she had naething to gie to the wee lassie but a little red calfy, and she telt the lassie whatever she wanted, the calfy would gie her. The king married again, an ill natured wife, wi'

three ugly dochters o' her ain. They did na like the little lassie because she was bonny; they took awa a' her braw claes that her ain mither had geen her, and put a rashin coatie on her, and gar't her sit in the kitchen neuk, and a' body ca'd her Rashin Coatie. She did na get ony thing to eat but what the rest left, but she did na care, for she went to her red calfy, and it gave her every thing she asked for. She got good meat from the calfy, but her ill natured step mother gart the calfy be killed, because it was good to Rashin Coatie. She was very sorry for the calfy, and sat down and grat. The dead calfy said to her,

> *'Tak me up, bane by bane*
> *And pit me aneth yon grey stane.*

And whatever you want, come and seek it frae me, and I will give you it.' Yuletide came, and a' the rest put on their braw claes, and was gaen awa to the kirk. Rashin Coatie said, 'oh I wad like to gang to the kirk too,' but the others said, 'what would you do at the kirk, you nasty thing? You must bide at home and make the dinner.' When they were gone to the kirk, Rashin Coatie did na ken how to make the dinner, but she went out to the grey stone, and she told the calfy that she could not make the dinner, and she wanted to win to the kirk. The calfy gave her braw claes, and bad her gang into the house, and say,

> *Every peat gar ither burn,*
> *Every spit gar ither turn,*
> *Every pot gar ither play*
> *Till I come frae the kirk this good Yule day.*

Rashin Coatie put on the braw claes that the calfy gave her, and went awa to the kirk, and she was the grandest and the brawest lady there. There was a young prince in the kirk and he fell in love with her. She cam awa before the blessing, and she was hame before the rest, and had off her braw claes, and had on her rashin coatie, and the calfy had covered the table, and the dinner was ready, and every thing in good order when the rest cam hame. The three sisters said to Rashin Coatie, 'oh lassie, if you had only seen the braw bonnie lady that was in kirk to day, that the young prince fell in love with.' She said 'oh I wish you would let me gang with you to the kirk tomorrow;' for they used to gang three days after ither to the kirk. They said, 'what should the like o' you do at the kirk, – nasty thing, – the kitchen neuk is good enough for you'. The next day they went away and left her, but she went back to her calfy, and he bade her repeat the same words as before, and he gave her brawer claes, and she went back to the kirk, and a' the world was looking at her, and wondering where sic a grand lady came from; and as for the young prince he fell more in love with her than ever, and bade some body watch where she went back to. But she was back afore any body saw her, and had off her braw claes and on her rashin coatie, and the calfy had the table covered, and every thing ready for the dinner.

The next day the calfy dressed her in brawer claes than ever, and she went back to the kirk. The young prince was there, and he put a guard at the door to keep her, but she jumped ower their heads and lost one of her beautiful satin slippers. She got home before the rest, and had on the rashin coatie, and the calfy had all things ready. The young prince put out a proclamation that he would marry whoever the satin slipper would fit. All the ladies of the land went to try on the slipper, and with the rest the three sisters, but none would it fit, for they had ugly broad feet. The hen wife took in her daughter, and cut her heels, and her toes, and the slipper was forced on her, and the prince must marry her, for he had to keep his promise. As he rode along, with her behind him, to be married, there was a bird began to sing and ever it sang,

> *Minched fit, and pinched fit*
> *Beside the king she rides,*
> *But braw fit, and bonny fit*
> *In the kitchen neuk she hides.*

The prince said, 'what is that the bird sings?' but the hen wife said, 'nasty lying thing! never mind what it says,' but the bird sang ever the same words. The prince said, 'oh, there must be some one that the slipper has not been tried on', but they said, 'there is none but a poor dirty thing that sits in the kitchen neuk, and wears a rashin coatie.' But the prince was determined to try it on Rashin Coatie, but she ran awa' to the grey stone, where the red calf dressed her yet brawer than ever, and she went to the prince, and the slipper jumped out of his pocket, and on to her foot, and the prince married her, and they lived happy all their days.

Mossycoat

Source: T. W. Thompson mss, notebook 7, pp. 55–72, Brotherton Library, University of Leeds. Narrated by Taimi Boswell at Oswaldtwistle, Lancashire, on 9 January 1915.

This magical version of 'The Dress of Gold, of Silver and of Stars' (AT510b) is one of more than ten stories noted by T. W. Thompson from the gypsy storyteller Taimi Boswell on this one day. Taimi introduced it as 'only but a few words'. Thompson's feat of recording so much of Taimi's repertoire over the four days 8–11 January 1915 is a great achievement: but without sound-recording equipment, compromises obviously had to be made. Thompson's solution was to make detailed plot outlines or summaries, noting all significant detail and trying to record phrases of unusual expressive force or importance.

The resulting text does not pretend to be a verbatim transcript of the storyteller's words. Nor does it convey much of the special flavour of the occasion, of the narrator's individual use of language, tone or gesture. It is, however, a faithful and reliable account of the story as told, and the reader sympathetic to Thompson's problems can I think reconstruct Taimi's narration from it.

The text printed here was written in fair copy at an uncertain date but fairly soon after the event into one of the numbered notebooks into which Thompson transcribed his folktale outlines. He intended at that time to expand each outline into more lively form, to convey the flavour as well as the substance of the individual narration. An expansion of 'Mossycoat' does exist, but this was written out about fifty years after the original narration. It is printed, with minor misreadings, in Katharine Briggs and Ruth Tongue, *The Folktales of England* and also in Briggs's *A Dictionary of British Folktales*.

However, the present text has a bare poetry that makes it even in outline state one of the most impressive narrations in the English folktale corpus. I have for ease of reading expanded ampersands and abbreviations; readers can supply definite articles where necessary. Otherwise I have corrected only a few obvious scribal errors (e.g. Thompson's first word is 'The' not 'There'). I have left in the text the confusion caused by Thompson's uncertainty about the mossycoat itself, but have incorporated in brackets his corrective notes identifying it as an undergarment that the girl never takes off.

The outline text proceeds at a steady pace in a non-committal past tense. Save in the formula 'it got on and it got on', Taimi Boswell's evidently subtle handling of time is not indicated. In the expanded text, there is considerable variation of tense depending on the emotional content of the event described. Once Mossycoat begins to act, and use her magic presents and powers, there is a shift of gear in the narrative from past to present tense. The story builds to a single focus, a point of intense and immediate concentration:

> She's in de ballroom now, Mossycoat is. De young master's bin waiting and watching for her. As soon as he sees her he exes his father to send for de fastest horse in his stable, and hev it kept standing ready saddled at de front door. Den he exes his mother to go over and talk to de young lady for a bit.

'De young lady' – Mossycoat – is a charmingly ruthless heroine: a working girl made good, rather than a princess revealed, despite her incongruous crown. The incest theme is submerged, with a nameless 'hawker' taking the lustful father's place.

THERE WAS A POOR old widow woman, who lived in a little cottage. She had two daughters, and younger, who was about nineteen or twenty, was very beautiful. The mother stored her like the heart in her belly. Mother was busy every day spinning a coat for her.

Hawker came courting this daughter, and was very much in love with her, and wanted to marry her. Girl was not in love with him, and didn't know what to do, so she consulted her mother. Mother told her to get what she could out of him whilst she was spinning her coat: when that was finished she would have no need of him or his presents. She told her daughter to say she would not marry him unless he would get her a dress made of white satin with sprigs of gold on it as big as a man's hand. This had to fit her exactly. Next time hawker came daughter told him this. He took good stock of her, and inside a week was back with dress. She and her mother went to try it on. It fit her exactly. She asked mother what she should do now. Mother said say you won't marry him unless he gets you a dress of silk and the colour of all the birds of the air. This too must fit exactly. Daughter told this to hawker. In two or three days he was back with dress. He knew size and fit by first. This one fit exactly. Daughter asked her mother what she should do now. Mother said say you won't marry him unless he gets you a pair of silver slippers, and they must fit exactly. Daughter told this to hawker, and in a few days he was back with slippers. Her foot was only about three inches long, but they fit her exactly – they was neither too loose nor too tight. Girl asked her mother what she should do now. Mother said she could finish her coat that night, so she might tell hawker she would marry him next day – he was to come at 10 o'clock. Daughter told her so-called lover this. 'Remember tomorrow, my dear, at 10 o'clock.' He would not forget, trust him.

That night mother was working late, but she finished coat. It was all made of green moss and gold thread. She christened it 'Mossycoat', and gave her daughter the same name. It was a magic coat, she said, and wherever the wearer wished herself to be there she would be, and whatever she wished to be it would be so.

Next morning she was up by it was light. She called her daughter, and said she must now go out into the world and seek her fortune, and a handsome fortune it was to be. She was a foreseer. She gave daughter the coat to take with her, and also a gold crown, and told her she must also take her two dresses and the silver slippers. She was to put Mossycoat on, and wish herself a hundred miles away. She was then to take it off, (* *She kept mossycoat on throughout under her other clothes*) carry it over her arm, and walk on till she came to a big hall. There she was to ask for work.

Daughter did as instructed and soon found herself in front of big gentleman's house. She asked for work. Mistress asked her what she could do: she liked the look of her. She was a very good cook, she said. Mistress said she could not give her job as cook as she already had one, but she would employ her to help cook if she was willing. Girl accepted this offer, so it was agreed that she should be under-cook. Mistress took her into kitchen, and announced this.

Mossycoat had none of her finery on: in fact she was in rags. Her mossycoat (*gold crown*) and her presents from hawker she hid away in her bedroom. When other servants saw her all in rags they made game of her. She was only fit to be scullery girl they said: they were better than her, and if anybody was to be under-cook it was one of them, not Mossycoat. So she had to scour the pans, and clean the knives and grates, etc. 'Pop, pop, pop,' down come the skimmer on her head. 'That's for you, Mossycoat. You'd be cook would you? That's what you'll get, and that's what you desarve, setting yourself above us.' So Mossycoat had to do all the dirty work, and was soon grease up to the ears, and as black as soot. And every now and then first one and then another would pop, pop, pop her over the head with the skimmer, till her head got so sore she could hardly bide.

It got on and it got on, and still Mossycoat was at her pans and grates, and still they were poping her over the head with the skimmer pop, pop, pop. Now there was a big dance coming on, and it was to last three nights. All the headmost people were going to be there, and of course the master and the mistress and their son – they only had one son – were going. This dance was all the talk among the servants: one was wishing she could be there, and another would like to dance with some of the young lords, and another would like to see the ladies' dresses, and so on: everybody would like to go, all save Mossycoat. If they only had the clothes to go in they would be all right they thought, for they all considered themselves as good as high titled ladies anyday. 'And, Mossycoat, you'd like to go, wouldn't you now, in all your rags and dirt? A fit person you to be there,' and then down come the skimmer, pop, pop, pop, on her poor head. And then they all laughed at her.

Now Mossycoat was very handsome, and rags and dirt couldn't hide this. The servants couldn't see it of course, but the young master had had his eyes on her, and the master and mistress always ta'en particular notice on her on account of her good looks. They thought when the time come it would be nice to ask her to go, and so sent for her, and did so. No, she would never think of such a thing: she knew her place better. She would greasy all one side of the coach etc., etc. They pressed her, but she definitely refused.

When she went back into the kitchen servants wanted to know what they had wanted her for – had she got notice? She said they had asked her to go to the ball. Well, that was beyond believing! Mossycoat would greasy all the men's clothes when she danced with them, if any would dance with her. The ladies would hold their noses as they passed her. She would be turned out etc., etc. If it had been any of them now – but Mossycoat the scullery girl! Then down came the skimmer on her head, pop, pop, pop.

Next night master, mistress and son asked her to go again, and said what a grand affair it had been the night before. She ought to have been there. They begged of her to go, especially the young master. She said about her grease, and dirt and rags etc., and positively declined. Servants were very sarcastic when she said that young master had wanted her to go specially, and down came skimmer on her head, pop, pop, pop.

That night Mossycoat thought she would go, unbeknown to everybody. She went and put on satin dress and silver shoes and gold crown, and mossycoat (*No. She put on Mossycoat under her rags,* and put servants under spell, and then put satin dress on over mossycoat. * Had M. on all time*). She touched servants without their noticing it, and they all fell fast asleep and under a spell. She wished herself there, and up she rose and away she went through the elements, and was there nearly as soon as words were out of her mouth.

The young gentleman sees her standing in ball-room: he had never seen anybody so handsome or so splendidly dressed before. He pestered his mother to know who she was. Mother didn't know. Couldn't she find out? Couldn't she go and talk to her? Mother saw he would never be at rest till she did go and talk to her. She went, and asked her various questions, who she was, where she came from etc., but all she could get out of her was that she came from the place where they hit her over the head with the skimmer. Presently young gentleman goes and asks her to have a dance with him. She refuses at first, but eventually consents. She dances once up and down room with him. He is madly in love with her. Then she says she must go. He presses her to stay, and when she won't, wants to see her off. But she just wishes herself back at home again, and there she is. He can't settle for rest of evening, and wants to go home.

When she gets back she finds the servants still asleep. She takes off satin dress, crown, and silver slippers, and then puts on her rags over her mossycoat. She then goes and touches servants, and they waken up at once. She threatens to tell mistress they have all been asleep all the evening. They beg her not to, and one gives her an old dress, another an old pair of stockings, another shoes, another stays if she won't. She promises not to, and this night they don't hit her over the head with the skimmer.

Next day the young gentleman is very unrestful. He can't settle his mind to anything. He does nothing but think of the mysterious girl with whom he has fallen in love at first sight. What could she mean by saying she came from where they hit her over the head with the skimmer? Would she be there to-night? The mother thought she was a very nice modest girl, but couldn't make out who she was or what she was.

Of course the servants got to hear about it, and were sarcastic over Mossycoat thinking young master wanted her to go specially, and skimmer came into use once more.

That night Mossycoat was again asked to go and again refused. Servants made merry over her. It was last chance she would have, etc., etc., and down came skimmer on head pop, pop, pop.

Mossycoat did exactly same as night before, except that she put on silk dress colours of all the birds of the air. Young gentleman had been waiting and watching for her appearance, and as soon as he saw her he sent his father to have fastest horse in stable brought and standing ready saddled at door. He then got his mother to go and talk to her a bit, but she discovered no more than night before. His horse had arrived now, so he went and asked her for dance. Everything same as night before, except that when she rushed out he did likewise, and jumped on his horse. She wished herself home, and rose in the elements and was there before she had closed her lips almost. In her fluster however she dropped one of the silver slippers. This young gentleman picked up, but as for catching her it was easier by far to catch the wind.

When she got home she did as night before. Servants offered her 1/-, 2/6, week's wages etc., not to tell and she promised she wouldn't.

Next day the young gentleman was ill in bed, he was dying for the love of the lady who had lost the silver slipper. Doctors could do him no good. It was given out what his state was, and that only the lady who could wear the silver slipper could save his life, and that her, if she could be found, he would marry. Ladies came from far and near, and some had big feet and some had small, but none had small enough to wear slipper, though they pinched and squeezed to get it on. Rich and poor came, but it was just the same. Of course all the servants tried but they were out of it altogether. The young gentleman was dying.

Was there nobody else at all? No, everybody had tried, except it was the scullery girl, Mossycoat. She must be brought, and brought she was. The slipper fitted her exactly. The young man jumped out of bed, and would have had her in his arms in a minute. 'Stop,' she said, and she ran off and appeared in her gold crown and satin dress, and the other silver slipper. Again he all but had her in his arms. 'Stop,' she said, and she ran off, and came back in her dress all the colours of the birds of the air. He nearly ate her. Then she told them about her mossy-coat.

There was just one thing. What did she mean when she said she came from the place where they hit her over the head with the skimmer? She explained – pop, pop, pop.

Well, all the servants were turned to the door and the dogs sent after them to drive them away. And Mossycoat and the young master got married, and she rode in her carriage and six, aye and ten if she wanted it, for you may be sure she had everything she wanted.

And they lived happy ever after, and had a basketful of children. I was there when the oldest son come of age, playing the fiddle, but that was many years since, and I shouldn't wonder if the old folks aren't dead by now, though I've never heard tell of it.

Dona Labismina

Source: Sílvio Roméro, *Contos Populares do Brazil*, (Lisbon, 1883; new ed. Rio de Janeiro, José Olympio, 1954). Told at Sergipe. Translated by Lourdes Gonçalves with Neil Philip.

This Brazilian 'Catskin' tale is notable for its unresolved ending, in which the happy forgetful bride fails to disenchant the snake-sister Labismina. This is individual to this telling. The snake which is coiled round the princess's neck when she is born is clearly a maternal guardian: though Labismina is referred to as the princess's 'sister', the honorific 'Dona', a title given only to married or mature and respected women, links her with the dead mother.

There is one puzzle in this narration, when the jewel the prince gives the disguised princess at the festival is later described as having been given to her 'at church'. The translator, Lourdes Gonçalves, tells me that in small towns in Brazil public festivals are held in the main square in front of the church, so it is possible that 'outside the church' is meant. It is just as likely, however, that this internal contradiction reflects a confusion of two Cinderella-variants, in one of which the meeting place is – as often in Catholic countries – the church.

Lourdes Gonçalves has made a literal translation which I have adapted to English idiom. My only substantive change is the introduction of the verb 'lash' to strengthen the final sentence.

ONCE UPON A TIME there was a queen who had been married for a long time but had never had a child. She longed for one so much that she wished, 'Please God let me give birth, if only to a snake!'

After a time, she became pregnant. When she did give birth, it was to a daughter, with a small snake coiled round her neck. All the family were very sorry, but they could not remove the snake from the child's neck.

They grew up together, and the girl was a fond friend of the little snake. When she became a young woman, she would stroll by the sea,

and the snake would leave her and play in the waves; but the princess would cry until the snake curled round her neck again. They would both return to the palace, and nobody knew anything about it.

This went on for some time. But one day the snake went into the sea and did not come back. The snake told her sister that whenever she was in danger she should call for her. The snake was called Labismina, and the princess, Maria.

Some years later, the queen fell ill and died. Before she died she took a ring from her finger and gave it to the king, saying, 'When you have to marry again, marry a princess whose finger fits this ring – not too slack and not too tight.' After some time, the king did want to get married, and he sent the ring to all the princesses of all the kingdoms: but for not one of them was the ring a true fit.

At last only Princess Maria, his daughter, had not tried the ring. The king called her and put the ring on her finger, and it fitted just right. So he told his daughter he would marry her. And when a king says something, it must be so.

Maria was so unhappy; she cried all the time. She went to Labismina by the sea shore; she cried for her, and the snake came. Maria told her what was wrong, and the snake told her: 'Don't be afraid. Tell the king that you will only marry him if he gives you a dress the colour of the field with all its flowers.'

The princess did as she was told, and the king was very upset. But he told her he would search for such a dress. And though it took him a long time, at last he found one.

Then the princess was sad once more, and went back to her sister, who told her, 'Tell him that you will only marry him if he gives you a dress the colour of the sea with all its fishes.'

The princess did as she was told, and the king was even more vexed than before. But though it took him a long time, at last he found one.

The young woman went again to Dona Labismina, who told her, 'Tell him that you will only marry him if he gives you a dress the colour of the sky with all its stars.'

She did as she was told, and this time the king was desperate, but he promised to look for it. He took even longer than before, but at last he got it.

When her father gave her the last dress, the princess thought she was lost, and she ran to the sea, where she boarded a ship which Dona Labismina had been preparing while the king looked for the dresses. Labismina told her sister to sail in the ship and land wherever it stopped, because she would marry the prince of that kingdom. And when she got married she should call three times for Labismina, so that she would be disenchanted, and become a princess too.

So Maria left, and where her ship stopped she went ashore. Because she had no means of living, she went to the queen to beg employment, and was put in charge of the king's hens.

After some time, there was a three-day festival in the town. Everyone in the palace went to the festival, and the poultry-maid stayed behind. But on the very first day, after everyone was gone, she combed her hair, put on her dress the colour of the field with all its flowers, asked Labismina for a beautiful carriage, and went to the festival herself. Everyone gaped in wonder to see such a pretty girl, so rich, and no one knew who she was. The prince, the king's son, soon fell deep in love with her. Before the festivities ended, the girl left, put on her old clothes, and went back to minding the hens.

As soon as they got back to the palace, the prince asked the queen, 'Mother, did you see what a lovely girl turned up at the festival today? I wish I could marry her! She looked just like our poultry-maid.'

'Don't say that, son: how could that poor girl have such fine, rich clothes? Go and look at her down there, all ragged and dirty.'

The prince went to the servant and told her, 'Poultry-maid, today at the festival I saw a girl who looked like you . . .'

'Oh! Prince, my lord, don't make fun of me. Who am I to be at the festival?'

On the next day there were more festivities, and the poultry-maid went to them secretly, in her dress the colour of the sea with all its fishes, in a still richer carriage. The prince fell even deeper in love, without knowing who she was.

On the third day, the same thing happened; the poultry-maid wore her dress the colour of the sky with all its stars. The prince was so enraptured that when he passed her he threw into her lap a jewel, which she kept.

When he got back to the palace, the prince was sick with love, and went to bed. He would not even sip his broth. The queen asked everyone to tempt him with broth, to see if he would take it, but it was no use. At last only the poultry-maid had not taken him any broth, and the queen told her to do so. She answered, 'Oh! Queen, are you making fun of me? Who am I, that the prince, my lord, would take broth from me? But I could prepare a broth to be sent to him.'

The queen agreed, and the servant prepared the cup of broth, and inside it she hid the jewel the prince had given her in church.

When the prince put his spoon in the broth and saw the jewel, he sprang happily from his bed, saying that he was quite cured, and that he wanted to marry the poultry-maid. She was sent for, and when she came, she was all dressed up as she had been at the festival.

There was great joy and feasting, and Princess Maria married the prince, but she forgot to call Labismina by name. So Labismina has never been freed from enchantment. That is why, even today, the sea still roars at times, and lashes itself into a fury.

La Sendraoeula

Source: Caterina Pigorini-Beri, 'La Cenerentola a Parma e a Camerino' in *Archivio per lo Studio delle Tradizioni Popolari*, Palermo, 1883. Translated by Nicoletta Simborowski.

This Italian story was collected by Caterina Pigorini-Beri from an old woman in Parma. She was originally from the village of Saragna, and was renowned for her storytelling skill. The collector was keenly aware of the need to provide strict unembellished records of oral narrations, and therefore retained such individual features as the narrator's variation between past and present tense, as well as scrupulously noting her dialect. As in 'Mossycoat', the narrator uses the variation of tense as a means of controlling the emotional pace of the tale.

The nonsense rhyme at the end is typical of Italian storytelling; the narrator was evidently not worried that the formulaic catch should be suited to the story which it closes. 'Confetti' in this context means sugared almonds, distributed as wedding sweets.

The opening of 'La Sendraoeula' will remind many readers of *King Lear*: not surprisingly, as *Lear* is itself based on a story derived from the Cinderella tradition, though Shakespeare transfers the central focus from the youngest daughter to her father. *King Lear*'s debt to Cinderella has been explored by Alan Dundes in his essay '"To Love My Father All": A Psychoanalytic Study of the Folktale Source of *King Lear*' in his *Cinderella: A Folklore Casebook*. Shakespeare's immediate source, Geoffrey of Monmouth's account of Lear in his twelfth-century *History of the Kings of Britain*, shows folktale transformed into pseudo-history.

THERE WAS ONCE a king, who had three daughters. The two oldest were jealous of the youngest, because she was prettier and kinder and the king loved her most; and they were afraid that he would marry her to someone from nearby and leave her the throne. They were always causing trouble and making her cross with their gossip and spite.

Every morning they would go and wish the king good day and ask him whether he had slept well.

Here I should tell you that he had three thrones: one white, one red and one black. When he was happy he sat on the white throne, when he was so-so he sat on the red one and when he was angry he sat on the black one.

One day he was so furious with the two oldest sisters that he sat on the black throne.

In the morning the firstborn goes to him and seeing him on the black throne says: 'Good day, father, sir, did you sleep well? Are you angry with me and is that why you are on the black throne?' And he says: 'Indeed I am angry.' 'But why?' asks the daughter. 'Because you don't really love me.' And she replies: 'I love you as much as eating chicken.' And then off she goes.

The other goes to him and says: 'Good day, father, sir, did you sleep well? Are you angry with me and is that why you are on the black throne?' 'Indeed,' says he, 'I am angry.' 'But why?' asks the daughter. 'Because you don't really love me.' And she replies: 'I love you as much as a piece of bread.' And then off she goes as well and the two of them plot to destroy the youngest and they say to her: 'Our father is angry with us because he says we don't really love him.' 'I told him,' adds the oldest, 'that I love him as much as eating chicken.' 'And I,' adds the other, 'told him that I love him as much as a piece of bread.'

The youngest, who was the most innocent and knew she was his favourite, says: 'I'll go and put him in a good humour: leave it to me and you'll see how we shall laugh.'

She goes to him and she too says: 'Good day, father, sir, did you sleep well? Are you angry with me and is that why you are on the black throne?' And he says immediately: 'Indeed I am angry because you don't really love me either.' 'I love you as much as a grain of salt.'

Then the king really is angry and, spurred on by those other two sisters, calls a servant and orders him to take the daughter into a wood, kill her and then bring her heart and clothing back home to him.

No sooner said than done, the servant seizes the girl, who was weeping like a cut vine, and takes her right into the wood.

But when they get there, his heart is so heavy at the idea of killing this innocent little girl, that he buys a sheep off a shepherd passing by, duly kills it, cuts out its heart and then strips the girl, and to cover her throws an ass's skin over her: then he finds a cleft willow-trunk to shelter her from the cold, puts her inside, goes home and delivers the heart and the clothing to the king, who is already regretting the order

he had given and falls into a great melancholy. But what was done was done and the two oldest sisters were merry as fishes.

At midnight, some witches are passing through the wood and ask her what she is doing in the cleft willow-trunk, cold as it is: and she tells them who she is and why she is in there: and so one of these witches gives her a wand and a little nut and tells her: 'Listen my child, when you need anything, tap this little nut with this wand, and see what you will get.'

Meanwhile, the king used to go hunting in the wood with his dog to keep himself amused. The dog had found his little mistress and every day took whatever he caught to her.

The king, who kept seeing the dog going off in the direction of the cleft willow, decided to follow him and see what there was there and he found this poor girl wearing an ass's skin who, so as not to betray the servant, told him that she had got lost in the wood and that she no longer had a home or roof over her head. The king was moved to pity and said that if she liked he would take her to his court to be kitchen-maid since they were just looking for a Cinderella; she said yes and he took her home.

Everyone received her kindly, especially the king. He could not forget his daughter and it seemed to him that this Cinderella looked like her.

It was the last few days of Carnival and his daughters were going to a ball at the prince's palace. The father, to divert his thoughts, accompanied them, all dressed in great finery. Cinderella let them go off, then she tapped the little nut with the wand and a lovely dress like the stars appeared, with golden shoes and stockings and a beautiful carriage-and-four. Then she too went to the ball.

When she arrived everyone danced with her, everyone wanted to accompany her home: but at midnight she insisted on leaving alone and said: 'I came all by myself and I want to leave by myself.' She climbed into the carriage and sped away.

The following morning her sisters said to her: 'Oh! You should have seen, Cinderella, what a beautiful lady there was at the ball, all dressed like the stars! Everyone danced with her, everyone wanted to escort her home.' And she murmured very quietly: 'That was me.' 'What did you say?' 'That I enjoyed myself more sitting here by the fire!'

The second time, she went wearing a dress like the sun. Everyone danced with her, everyone wanted to be near her, and the prince was already well and truly in love with her. But she kept telling him that she could not say anything and kept him at bay with fine words so as not to give herself away. He had guards put at the doors so that she couldn't escape, but she said: 'I came all by myself and I want to leave by myself,' and she threw handfuls of confetti so that they were blinded and could not see where she had gone.

In the morning, her sisters said to her: 'You should have seen, Cinderella, that lady all dressed like the sun: everyone wanted to see where she had gone but she threw confetti and blinded the guards.' And she replied: 'That was me.' 'What did you say?' 'That I enjoyed myself more sitting here by the fire!'

The third time she went wearing a dress like the moon, but she was made to dance so much that midnight went by without her realizing, and that was the time when she had to be back home by the fire, otherwise the spell would not work any more. She said: 'I came all by myself and I want to leave by myself,' and she started to run home, because this time the prince wanted to chase after her himself. She threw down a great heap of flowers and managed to escape this time too, but as she climbed into the carriage, without realizing, she lost a golden shoe and this was taken to the prince. She rushed home to get undressed, but in her haste she forgot to take off her golden stockings.

As soon as her sisters came home they said to her: 'You should have seen, Cinderella, that lovely lady, all dressed like the moon: everyone chased after her, but she escaped and lost a golden shoe.'

And she said: 'That was me!' 'What did you say?' 'That I enjoyed myself more sitting here by the fire.'

In the morning the prince published an edict that he would marry the woman that the golden shoe fitted; and straightaway, tootoo, tootoo, tootoo with the trumpet, they're off round the whole town, going into all the houses trying on the shoe, but it was so tiny that it didn't fit any woman. So they went to the king's palace too. The two daughters try it on, but they couldn't even get their big toe in it, and so for a joke they say: 'Let's try it on Cinderella.' She remembered that she had not taken off her golden stockings and didn't want to have anything to do with it: but partly to make the king laugh they force her to try it on and discover the golden stockings.

Then the father, delighted to have got his daughter back alive, gave her in marriage to the prince and had her carried in triumph throughout the city. Eventually she became queen and her two sisters were furious as dogs: and they made a cake and a pie and didn't even give me a piece to try.

The Poor Turkey Girl

Source: Frank Hamilton Cushing, *Zuñi Folk Tales*, New York and London, G. P. Putnam's Sons, The Knickerbocker Press, 1901.

Frank Hamilton Cushing (1857–1900) took his ethnological studies of the Zuñi Indians of New Mexico so far as to become a Zuñi priest, with the name Medicine Flower.

In the introduction to the 1931 reissue of his collection of Zuñi folktales, Mary Austin vehemently denies that this story is a Zuñi adaptation of Cinderella. She writes, 'The Turkey Girl is a favourite character in all Pueblo fiction . . . To one familiar with the movements of the Amerind mind the Turkey Girl is a transcript of the experience of the loss of reality by indulgence in the day-dream.' However the folktale scholar Stith Thompson, who made a special study of American Indian tales, had no doubt that 'Poor Turkey Girl' is, as it seems to be, a Cinderella variant, despite its sad ending.

Cinderella stories have been collected from a number of American Indian tribes: one of the most affecting was collected from the Canadian Micmacs by Cyrus Macmillan and published in his *Canadian Wonder Tales* as 'The Indian Cinderella'. In it, 'Strong Wind, the Invisible' announces that he will marry the first girl who can see him as he comes home at night. The two eldest daughters of the chief both lie in an attempt to win him; their sister, whom they cruelly mistreat, is truthful, does see him, and marries him. But as for the sisters, 'he changed them both into aspen trees and rooted them in the earth. And since that day the leaves of the aspen have always trembled, and they shiver in fear at the approach of Strong Wind, it matters not how softly he comes, for they are still mindful of his great power and anger because of their lies and their cruelty to their sister long ago.'

LONG LONG AGO, our ancients had neither sheep nor horses nor cattle; yet they had domestic animals of various kinds – amongst them Turkeys.

In Mátsaki, or the Salt City, there dwelt at this time many very wealthy families, who possessed large flocks of these birds, which it was their custom to have their slaves or the poor people of the town herd in the plains round about Thunder Mountain, below which their town stood, and on the mesas beyond.

Now in Mátsaki at this time there stood, away out near the border of the town, a little tumbledown, single-room house, wherein there lived alone a very poor girl, – so poor that her clothes were patched and tattered and dirty, and her person, on account of long neglect and ill-fare, shameful to look upon, though she herself was not ugly, but had a winning face and bright eyes; that is, if the face had been more oval and the eyes less oppressed with care. So poor was she that she herded Turkeys for a living; and little was given to her except the food she subsisted on from day to day, and perhaps now and then a piece of old, worn-out clothing.

Like the extremely poor everywhere and at all times, she was humble, and by her longing for kindness, which she never received, she was made kind even to the creatures that depended upon her, and lavished this kindness upon the Turkeys she drove to and from the plains every day. Thus, the Turkeys, appreciating this, were very obedient. They loved their mistress so much that at her call they would unhesitatingly come, or at her behest go whithersoever and whensoever she wished.

One day this poor girl, driving her Turkeys down into the plains, passed near Old Zuñi, – the Middle Ant Hill of the World, as our ancients have taught us to call our home, – and as she went along, she heard the herald-priest proclaiming from the house-top that the Dance of the Sacred Bird (which is a very blessed and welcome festival to our people, especially to the youths and maidens who are permitted to join in the dance) would take place in four days.

Now, this poor girl had never been permitted to join in or even to watch the great festivities of our people or the people in the neighbouring towns, and naturally she longed very much to see this dance.

But she put aside her longing, because she reflected: 'It is impossible that I should watch, much less join in the Dance of the Sacred Bird, ugly and ill-clad as I am.' And thus musing to herself and talking to her Turkeys, as was her custom, she drove them on, and at night returned them to their cages round the edges and in the plazas of the town.

Every day after that, until the day named for the dance, this poor girl, as she drove her Turkeys out in the morning, saw the people busy in cleaning and preparing their garments, cooking delicacies, and otherwise making ready for the festival to which they had been duly invited by the other villagers, and heard them talking and laughing merrily at the prospect of the coming holiday. So, as she went about with her Turkeys through the day, she would talk to them, though she never dreamed that they understood a word of what she was saying.

It seems that they did understand even more that she said to them, for on the fourth day, after the people of Mátsaki had all departed toward Zuñi and the girl was wandering around the plains alone with her Turkeys, one of the big Gobblers strutted up to her, and making a fan of his tail, and skirts, as it were, of his wings, blushed with pride and puffed with importance, stretched out his neck, and said: 'Maiden mother, we know what your thoughts are, and truly we pity you, and wish that, like the other people of Mátsaki, you might enjoy this holiday in the town below. We have said to ourselves at night, after you have placed us safely and comfortably in our cages: "Truly our maiden mother is as worthy to enjoy these things as any one in Mátsaki, or even Zuñi." Now listen well, for I speak the speech of all the elders of my people: If you will drive us in early this afternoon, when the dance is most gay and the people are most happy, we will help you to make yourself so handsome and so prettily dressed that never a man, woman, or child amongst all those who are assembled at the dance will know you; but rather, especially the young men, will wonder whence you came, and long to lay hold of your hand in the circle that forms round the altar to dance. Maiden mother, would you like to go to see this dance, and even join in it, and be merry with the best of your people?'

The poor girl was at first surprised. Then it seemed all so natural that the Turkeys should talk to her as she did to them, that she sat down on a little mound, and leaning over, looked at them and said: 'My beloved Turkeys, how glad I am that we may speak together! But why should you tell me of things that you full well know I so long to, but cannot by any possible means, do?'

'Trust in us,' said the old Gobbler, 'for I speak the speech of my people, and when we begin to call and call and gobble, and turn toward our home in Mátsaki, do you follow us, and we will show you what we can do for you. Only let me tell you one thing: No one knows how much happiness and good fortune may come to you if you but enjoy temperately the pleasures we enable you to participate in. But if, in the excess of your enjoyment, you should forget us, who are your friends, yet so much depend upon you, then we will think: "Behold, this our maiden mother, though so humble and poor, deserves, forsooth, her hard life, because, were she more prosperous, she would be unto others as others now are unto her."'

'Never fear, O my Turkeys,' cried the maiden, – only half trusting that they could do so much for her, yet longing to try, – 'never fear. In everything you direct me to do I will be obedient as you always have been to me.'

The sun had scarce begun to decline when the Turkeys of their own accord turned homeward, and the maiden followed them, light of heart. They knew their places well, and immediately ran to them. When all had entered, even their barelegged children, the old Gobbler called to the maiden, saying: 'Enter our house.' She therefore went in. 'Now, maiden sit down,' said he, 'and give to me and my companions, one by one, your articles of clothing. We will see if we cannot renew them.'

The maiden obediently drew off the ragged old mantle that covered her shoulders and cast it on the ground before the speaker. He seized it in his beak, and spread it out, and picked and picked at it; then he trod upon it, and lowering his wings, began to strut back and forth over it. Then taking it up in his beak, and continuing to strut, he puffed and puffed, and laid it down at the feet of the maiden, a beautiful white embroidered cotton mantle. Then another Gobbler came forth, and she gave him another article of dress, and then another and another, until each garment the maiden had worn was new and as beautiful as any possessed by her mistresses in Mátsaki.

Before the maiden donned all these garments, the Turkeys circled about her, singing and singing, and clucking and clucking, and brushing her with their wings, until her person was as clean and her skin as smooth and bright as that of the fairest maiden of the wealthiest home in Mátsaki. Her hair was soft and wavy, instead of being an ugly, sun-burnt shock; her cheeks were full and dimpled, and her eyes dancing, with smiles, – for she now saw how true had been the words of the Turkeys.

Finally, one old Turkey came forward and said: 'Only the rich ornaments worn by those who have many possessions are lacking to thee, O maiden mother. Wait a moment. We have keen eyes, and have gathered many valuable things, – as such things, being small though precious are apt to be lost from time to time by men and maidens.'

Spreading his wings, he trod round and round upon the ground, throwing his head back, and laying his wattled beard on his neck; and, presently beginning to cough, he produced in his beak a beautiful necklace; another Turkey brought forth earrings, and so on, until all the proper ornaments appeared, befitting a well-clad maiden of the olden days, and were laid at the feet of the poor Turkey girl.

With these beautiful things she decorated herself, and, thanking the Turkeys over and over, she started to go, and they called out: 'O maiden mother, leave open the wicket, for who knows whether you will remember your Turkeys or not when your fortunes are changed, and if you will not grow ashamed that you have been the maiden mother of Turkeys? But we love you, and would bring you to good fortune. Therefore, remember our words of advice, and do not tarry too long.'

'I will surely remember, O my Turkeys!' answered the maiden.

Hastily she sped away down the river path toward Zuñi. When she arrived there, she went in at the western side of the town and through one of the long covered ways that lead into the dance court. When she came just inside of the court, behold, every one began to look at her, and many murmurs ran through the crowd, – murmurs of astonishment at her beauty and the richness of her dress, – and the people were all asking one another, 'Whence comes this beautiful maiden?'

Not long did she stand there neglected. The chiefs of the dance, all gorgeous in their holiday attire, hastily came to her, and, with apologies for the incompleteness of their arrangements, – though these arrangements were as complete as they possibly could be, – invited her to join the youths and maidens dancing round the musicians and the altar in the center of the plaza.

With a blush and a smile and a toss of her hair over her eyes, the maiden stepped into the circle, and the finest youths among the dancers vied with one another for her hand. Her heart became light and her feet merry, and the music sped her breath to rapid coming and going, and the warmth swept over her face, and she danced and danced until the sun sank low in the west.

But, alas! in the excess of her enjoyment, she thought not of her Turkeys, or if she thought of them, she said to herself, 'How is this, that I should go away from the most precious consideration to my flock of gobbling Turkeys? I will stay a while longer, and just before the sun sets I will run back to them, that these people may not see who I am, and that I may have the joy of hearing them talk day after day and wonder who the girl was who joined in their dance.'

So the time sped on, and another dance was called, and another, and never a moment did the people let her rest; but they would have her in every dance as they moved around the musicians and the altar in the center of the plaza.

At last the sun set, and the dance was well-nigh over, when, suddenly breaking away, the girl ran out, and, being swift of foot, – more so than most of the people of her village, – she sped up the river path before any one could follow the course she had taken.

Meantime, as it grew late, the Turkeys began to wonder and wonder that their maiden mother did not return to them. At last a gray old Gobbler mournfully exclaimed, 'It is as we might have expected. She has forgotten us; therefore is she not worthy of better things than those she has been accustomed to. Let us go forth to the mountains and endure no more of this irksome captivity, inasmuch as we may no longer think our maiden mother as good and true as once we thought her.'

So, calling and calling to one another in loud voices, they trooped out of their cage and ran up toward the Cañon of the Cottonwoods, and then round behind Thunder Mountain, through the Gateway of Zuñi, and so on up the valley.

All breathless, the maiden arrived at the open wicket and looked in. Behold, not a Turkey was there! Trailing them, she ran and she ran up the valley to overtake them; but they were far ahead, and it was only after a long time that she came within the sound of their voices, and then, redoubling her speed, well-nigh overtook them, when she heard them singing this song:

> *K'yaanaa, to! to!*
> *K'yaanaa, to! to!*
> *Ye ye!*
> *K'yaanaa, to! to!*
> *K'yannaa, to! to!*
> *Yee huli huli!*

The Poor Turkey Girl

Hon awen Tsita
Itiwanakwïn
   Otakyaan aaa kyaa;
Lesna akyaaa
Shoya-k'oskwi
Teyäthltokwïn
   Hon aawani!

   Ye yee huli huli,
   Tot-tot, tot-tot, tot-tot,
     Huli huli!
   Tot-tot, tot-tot, tot-tot,
     Huli huli!

Up the river, *to! to!*
Up the river, *to! to!*
   Sing *ye ye!*
Up the river, *to! to!*
Up the river, *to! to!*
   Sing *yee huli huli!*

Oh, our maiden mother
To the Middle Place
   To dance went away;
Therefore as she lingers,
To the Cañon Mesa
And the plains above it
   We all run away!

Sing *ye yee huli huli,*
   Tot-tot, tot-tot, tot-tot,
     Huli huli!
   Tot-tot, tot-tot, tot-tot,
     Huli huli!'

Hearing this, the maiden called to her Turkeys; called and called in
vain. They only quickened their steps, spreading their wings to help
them along, singing the song over and over until, indeed, they came to
the base of the Cañon Mesa, at the borders of the Zuñi Mountains.
Then singing once more their song in full chorus, they spread wide

their wings, and *thlakwa-a-a*, *thlakwa-a-a*, they fluttered away over the plains above.

The poor Turkey girl threw her hands up and looked down at her dress. With dust and sweat, behold! it was changed to what it had been, and she was the same poor Turkey girl that she was before. Weary, grieving, and despairing, she returned to Mátsaki.

Thus it was in the days of the ancients. Therefore, where you see the rocks leading up to the top of Cañon Mesa (Shoya-k'oskwi), there are the tracks of turkeys and other figures to be seen. The latter are the song that the Turkeys sang, graven in the rocks; and all over the plains along the borders of Zuñi Mountains since that day turkeys have been more abundant than in any other place.

After all, the gods dispose of men according as men are fitted; and if the poor be poor in heart and spirit as well as in appearance, how will they be aught but poor to the end of their days?

Thus shortens my story.

The Boy and his Stepmother

Source: A. Campbell, *Santal Folk Tales*, Pokhuria, Santal Mission Press, 1891.

This sardonic little tale is unusual in its mickey-taking conclusion, but not in its male protagonist. Other Indian variants with male Cinderellas can be found for instance in C. H. Bodding, *Folklore of the Santal Parganas*, and A. E. Dracott, *Simla Village Tales*. 'The Boy and his Stepmother' was collected and translated by A. Campbell, of the Free Church of Scotland Santal Mission. It was first published in the *Indian Evangelical Review*, October 1886.

Seeking out a spouse through a randomly cast hair is here the equivalent of the chance-found shoe. It will inevitably remind Western readers of the story of King Mark and Iseult; in other Indian tales the long beautiful hair is shed by a woman. This motif can be found in one of the earliest recorded folktales, the Egyptian 'Anpu and Bata', or 'The Two Brothers', preserved in a papyrus dating from about 1250 BC.

A CERTAIN BOY had charge of a cow which he used to tend while grazing. One day the cow said to him, 'How is it that you are becoming so emaciated?' The boy replied, 'My stepmother does not give me sufficient food.' The cow then said to him, 'Do not tell any one, and I will give you food. Go to the jungle and get leaves with which to make a plate and cup.' The boy did as he was ordered, and behold, the cow from one horn shook boiled rice into the leaf plate, and from the other a relish for the rice into the cup. This continued daily for a considerable time, until the boy became sleek and fat.

The stepmother came to know of the relation which existed between the cow and her herd-boy, and to be revenged upon them she feigned illness. To her attendants she said, 'I cannot possibly live.' They asked, 'What would make you live?' She replied, 'If you kill the cow, I will recover.' They said, 'If killing the cow will cure you, we will kill it.' The boy hearing that the life of the cow which supplied him with food was threatened, ran to her and said, 'They are about to kill you.' Hearing this the cow said, 'You go and make a rope of rice straw, make some parts thick, and some thin, and put it in such a place as they can easily find it. When they are about to kill me, you seize hold of my tail and pull.' The next day they proceeded to make arrangements to kill the cow, and finding the rope prepared by the boy the day before, they tied her with it to a stake. After she was tied the boy laid hold of her tail, and pulled so that the rope by which she was secured was made taut. A man now raised an axe, and felled her by a blow on the forehead. As the cow staggered the rope broke, and she and the boy were borne away on the wind, and alighted in an unexplored jungle. From the one cow other cows sprang, in number equal to a large herd, and from them another large herd was produced. The boy then drove his two herds of cows to a place where they could graze, and afterwards took them to the river to drink. The cows having quenched their thirst, lay down to rest, and the boy bathed, and afterwards combed and dressed his hair. During this latter operation a hair from his head fell into the river, and was carried away by the current.

Some distance lower down, a princess with her female companions and attendants came to bathe. While the princess was in the water she noticed the hair floating down stream, and ordered some one to take it out, which when done they measured, and found it to be twelve cubits long. The princess on returning home went to the king, her father, and showing him the hair she had found in the river said, 'I have made up my mind to marry the man to whom this hair belonged.' The king gave his consent, and commanded his servants to search for the object of his daughter's affection. They having received the king's command went to a certain barber and said to him, 'You dress the hair and beards of all the men in this part of the country, tell us where the man with hair twelve cubits long is to be found.' The barber, after many days, returned unsuccessful. The king's servants after a long consultation as to whom they should next apply to, decided upon laying the matter before a tame parrot belonging to the king. Going to the parrot they said, 'Oh parrot, can you find the man whose hair is twelve cubits long?' The parrot replied, 'Yes, I can find him.' After flying here and there the parrot was fortunate enough to find the boy. It was evening, and having driven his two herds of cattle into their pen, he had sat down, and was employed in dressing his long hair. His flute was hanging on a bush by his side.

The parrot sat awhile considering how she might take him to the king's palace. Seeing the flute the idea was suggested to her, that by means of it she might contrive to lead him where she desired. So taking it up in her beak, she flew forward a little and alighted in a small bush. To regain possession of his flute the boy followed, but on his approach the bird flew away, and alighted on another bush a short distance ahead. In this way she continued to lead him by flying from bush to bush until at length she brought him to the king's palace. He was then brought before his majesty, and his hair measured, and found to be twelve cubits in length. The king then ordered food to be set before him, and after he was refreshed the betrothal ceremony was performed.

As it was now late they prevailed upon him to pass the night as the guest of the king. Early in the morning he set out, but, as he had a long distance to go, the day was far advanced before he reached the place where his cattle were. They were angry at having been kept penned up to so late an hour, and as he removed the bars to let them out, they knocked him down, and trampled upon his hair in such a way, as to pull it all out leaving him bald. Nothing daunted, he collected his cows, and started on his return journey, but as he drove them along, one after another vanished, so that only a few remained when he reached the king's palace.

On his arrival they noticed that he had lost all his hair, and on being questioned he related to the king all that had fallen him. His hair being gone the princess refused to marry him, so instead of becoming the king's son-in-law, he became one of his hired servants.

The Finger Lock

Source:*Tocher* 1, Edinburgh, School of Scottish Studies, 1971. Recorded from Andra 'Hoochten' Stewart, Blairgowrie, Perthshire, by Hamish Henderson, August 1955. Tape reference SA1955/153 A3.

This well-known tale is an example of a legend attached to a particular family, explaining the origin of a particular tune, shaping itself round an international tale type. The MacCrimmons were the hereditary pipers of the MacLeods of Dunvegan in Skye.

In a nineteenth-century Gaelic version of this story in James Mac-Dougall's *Folk Tales and Fairy Lore*, the youngest brother is known as the Black Lad MacCrimmon. He is 'kept down by the rest, and left to do every piece of work that was more slavish than another'. The fairy who comes to him offers him the choice in music between 'skill without success, or success without skill'.

Andra Stewart says of his version, 'That was ma father told me that an he played that tune on the pipes, aul John Stewart, the piper, played that pibroch. Aa haven't got the chanter now, or aa cuid ha played a bit o't masael tae ye.'

THIS IS A STORY about the MacCrimmons. There was three brothers of the MacCrimmons, an they lived in a cottage away on a hill. An the two oldest ones was very good pipers, an the youngest one couldnae play the pipes at aa. They jist kep him for a slave in the hous, fir sweepin the flair, washin the dishes an making meat fir them.

So houiver, there wes a great Games came off, jist like Braemar, there wes Games like Braemar in them days, ye see, an the brothers says, 'Well, we'll have to get aa wir belts an buckles an ivrything shined up, an our medals, for the Games tomorrow, an git wir pipes tuned up.' So the youngest yin, he's washin the dishes as usual, an he says, 'Geordie,' he says, 'Wull ye let me go to the Games wi yeze the morn? Aa've niver been at the Games in ma life, an aa'd like to see yeze playin, an aa'd like to see aa these gret pipers that comes frae aa these islands,' he says, 'playin at the Games.'

'Away an be quiet, laddie,' he says, an he drew his haun an he hut his young brother a slap in the face. 'Git on wi the work thair,' he says, 'ye've the cou tae hird,' he says, 'doun to the burn-side. Ye've sticks tae break up,' he says, 'an the byre tae clean oot,' he says. 'We've nae time to take you in the mess ye are,' he says, 'to the Games to see pipers playin,' he says.

Well, he was aafie broken-hertit, he wes down in the mouth because he couldnae git away wi his brothers. They were oot the next day, an they went in their trap an horse, an got their pipe-boxes an that in the back o the trap, an they drove off, gien him aa that he had to dae, the young laddie, tellt him aa that he had to dae when they were away. So he wes doun at the burn-side an he's lyin thinkin, an his cou's eating up and doun the burn-side, an he hears a wee voice sayin tae him, 'Whit's wrang wi ye,' he says, 'Johnnie? Ye're aafie doun-hertit lookin.' Aw, he looks doun at this, an this wes a wee fairy, a wee green man at the burn's side, sittin platt-leggit, lookin at him. He says, 'Aa've asked ma brothers,' he says, 'to see if aa could git wi them to the Games,' he says. 'Aa nivver seen the Games in ma life,' he says, 'an they wunnae let me. Aa they keep me fur is fir slavin in the hous, making me dae this, dae that, Johnnie, dae this, Johnnie,' he says, 'that's aa the good aa git,' he says. 'Aa nivver see the Games, an,' he says, 'Wan o them hut me.'

'Nivver mind,' says the fairy, he says, 'aa'll play ye a tune or two.'

'Bit,' he says, 'whayr's the pipes?'

He says, 'Aa've nae pipes tae play on,' he says. 'Aa dinnae need pipes, Johnnie,' he says, 'aa'll jist tak a winnle-strae aff the bank,' he says, 'an that'll make the pipes fir the fairies.'

So the wee green man sat down beside him an pit the strae in its mouth, an it played the loveliest strathspeys an reels, iver ye heard the like o on the strae. 'Now,' says the fairy, he says, 'Aa dinnae want to keep ye too long,' he says. 'You go up,' he says, 'to the hous and get yersel dressed, get yer pipes,' he says, 'an ye'll catch the Games yet.' He says, 'You can play better 'n that.'

'No me,' says Johnnie, he says, 'Aa cannae even gie a tune on the chanter,' he says, 'Aa cannae play nane.' 'Yes,' he says, 'ye'll play. Ye come on up wi me quick,' he says, 'or ye'll no hae time,' he says 'the cou'll be aa right, aa'll watch the cou tae ye come back.'

Up they goes, an the laddie, wee Johnnie says, 'Aw bit they locked the door,' says Johnnie, he says, 'Aa'll no git in. They take the key wi them an they lock me oot in case aa eat onie meat or anything in the hous.' 'Jist blow yir breath on the lock, an put yir wee finger into the lock,' he says, 'an gie'd a turn an ye'll open the door.' So Johnnie went forrit an he blew his breath on the lock o the door, an he pit his wee finger in the lock o the door an gies his wee finger a turn, an the door opent. Whan they cam in, the fairy cam in wi him, an says, 'Go ben the room, Johnnie, an pull that auld kist frae aneath the bed.' Johnnie says, 'Where's the aul kist?' 'Ben the room,' he says, 'go and pull it oot.' He went ben the room, an he pulls this aul kist, an it wes all cobwebs an stoor, this aul kist. An he lifts the lid aff the kist, there wes the pipes, gold-mountit pipes, solid gold. Kilts, ivrything, ye nivver seen the like o them.

The fairy helps to dress him, gies him the golden pipes. 'Now,' he says, 'tune yir pipes before ye go away.' Johnnie says, 'Aa cannae go to the Games,' he says, 'Aa'm tellin ye aa cannae play.' 'Aye,' he says, 'aa hear ye.' Johnnie pit the pipes on his shoulder an he tunet up. Ye've never heard a piper – to this day there's never been a piper in Scotland like him, this Johnnie. He played, an he couldnae stop. 'Now,' says the fairy, 'that'll dae,' he says, 'ye cannae play any longer strathspeys an reels an pibroch. Now,' he says, 'thir's one pibroch aa want ye to play,' he says, 'an that's THE FINGER LOCK.' He says, 'Ye blew yir breath on the lock o the door, an ye'll come in here an ye'll pit yir wee finger on, an thair's a tune,' he says, 'an that's the name ye'll cry it, this new pibroch,' he says, 'ye'll play it. Jist work yir fingers when ye go on to the stage,' he says, 'an ye'll play THE FINGER LOCK.' If they ask ye what name the pibroch is, that's the name you've got to tell them, THE FINGER LOCK.'

Johnnie says, 'Aa right.' He got the trap an got his horse – another horse yokit, an he's in. He wes jist rushin, he was rushin doun to git to the Games, he wes the last piper on the stage, an whan he went on ivirybody sat jist in a dream lookin at him. Strathspeys an reels an his pibroch, an he played this new pibroch, an the judges come forrit an he says, 'Aye,' said the judge, 'my man, you can play!' He says, 'What pibroch's that?' he says. 'THE FINGER LOCK,' he says. 'Sir,' he says, 'That's the new pibroch,' he says, 'ma own composin.'

But the fairy told him that he leave before his brothers cam home, because the brothers wad be haein a drink . . . before he would come hame. He got into the cairt, this trap, an he drove home. Pit ivrything back in the kist an shoved it beneath the bed an he's in his old rags again, he's sweepin an sweepin away at the hous an cleanin up, whan this two brothers cam in. They cam in totterin an tired-lookin. They left their pipes doun an they're sat doun an they're speakin to thirsels, speakin aboot, 'Thon wes a good piper – ha-a, we niver seen a piper like thon. Aa'll niver go t' the Games, thir's a lot mair o's will niver go t' the Games,' an that's the wey they wir going on, ye see. An Johnnie's laughin to his-sel an he's lissnin to thum. So he turns roun an he says, 'How did yeze git on the day, brothers? Did yiz get oniething?' 'Get oniething!' he says, 'You couldn't play wi a man like thon,' he says, 'not,' he says, 'thir not a piper,' he says, 'in the world'll beat thon man at playin. Aa niver heard a piper like thon in ma life.'

'What kind a piper wiz he?'

'He played a tune,' he says, 'THE FINGER LOCK,' he says, 'the pibroch,' he says, 'aa niver heard the like o thon,' he says.

'THE FINGER LOCK,' says Johnnie. 'Good Gode man,' he says, 'Aa cuid play that tune masel.'

'Away, ye sullie laddie!' The auldest brother made a kick at him. 'Get oot o the road,' he says, 'an no be sullie,' he says, 'ye're daft, man.'

'Aw well,' says Johnnie, he says. 'Gimme yir pipes,' he says, 'Aa'll pley THE FINGER LOCK tae ye.' So he went owre.

'Lea ma pipes alane!'

'All right,' says Johnnie, 'Aa'll get ma ain pipes.'

So he walks ben the room an he lufts the golden-mountit pipes, an he comes throu the hous. He comes throu the hous, an he tunes up his pipes, an the two brothers suttin, lookt at him playin, an they jist sutt wi thir mooths open, watchin their brither playin. An from that day to this, the two oldest brothers niver went to thir Games. It wes Johnnie that went, an luftit, swep the boards, ivry place he's went, an that pibroch gits played to this day yit. THE FINGER LOCK's the name o the pibroch, an that's whae it came aff o, the MacCrimmons, the three brithers o the MacCrimmons.

An if you ask a piper, a good piper that goes to the Games, to play THE FINGER LOCK, a pibroch, ye'll hear them playin it. An that's true.

The Bracket Bull

Source: Douglas Hyde, *Four Irish Stories*, Dublin, 1898. Translated from the Gaelic by Douglas Hyde (An Chraoibhin Aoibhinn); the original text can be found in Hyde's *Sgeuluidhe Gaodhalach*.

Hyde's note tells us that 'I wrote this story carefully down, word for word, from the telling of two men – the first, Shawn Cunningham of Ballinphuil, and the second, Martin Brennan of Ballinlocha, in the barony of Frenchpark. They each told the same story, but Martin Brennan repeated the end of it at greater length than the other. The first half is written down word for word from the mouth of Cunningham, the second half from that of Brennan.' The style of narration, with the strings of epithets, the formulaic phrases, the relish for language and incident, is typical of much Gaelic storytelling.

'The Bracket Bull' is a version of 'The Little Red Ox' (AT511a), the male equivalent of 'One-Eye, Two-Eyes and Three-Eyes'. There are a number of Balkan, Irish and Scandinavian texts, of which the best known are 'Katie Woodencloak' in Asbjornsen and Moe's *Popular Tales from the Norse* (though this version has a heroine) and the English gypsy version collected by John Sampson, 'De Little Bull-Calf', which, like 'The Bracket Bull' merges 'The Little Red Ox' with the 'Dragon-Slayer' tale type (AT300).

Usually in 'The Dragon-Slayer', the hero proves his feat by producing the tongue of the dragon he has killed; here, the Cinderella shoe-test makes a surprise appearance.

'Caher' is glossed by Hyde as 'stone fort or rampart or castle'.

THERE WAS A MAN in it [*i.e.* alive] long ago, and long ago it was, and if he was in it then he would not be in it now. He was married and his wife was lost [*i.e.* died], and he had only one son by the first wife. Then he married the second wife. This second wife had not much regard for the son, and he was obliged to go out on the mountain, far from the house to take care of the cattle.

There was a bracket [speckled] bull amongst the cows out on the mountain, and of a day that there was great hunger on the lad the bracket bull heard him complaining and wringing his two hands, and he moved over to him and said to him: 'You are hungry, but take the horn off me and lay it on the ground; put your hand into the place where the horn was and you will find food.'

When he heard that he went over to the bull, took hold of the horn, twisted it, and it came away with him in his hand. He laid it on the ground, put in his hand and drew out food and drink and a tablecloth. He spread the tablecloth on the ground, set the food and drink on it, and then he ate and drank his enough. When he had his enough eaten and drunk he put the tablecloth back again, and left the horn back in the place where it was before.

When he came home that evening he did not eat a bit of his supper, and his stepmother said to herself that he [must have] got something to eat out on the mountain since he was not eating any of his supper.

When he went out with his cattle the next day his stepmother sent her own daughter out after him, and told her to be watching him till she would see where he was getting the food. The daughter went and put herself in hiding and she was watching him until the heat of the day came: but when the middle of the day was come she heard every music more excellent than another, and she was put to sleep by that truly melodious music. The bull came then, and the lad twisted the horn off him, and drew out the tablecloth, the food, and the drink, and ate and drunk his enough. He put back the horn again then. The music was stopped and the daughter woke up, and was watching him until the evening came, and he drove the cows home then. The mother asked her did she see anything in the field, and she said that she did not. The lad did not eat two bites of his supper, and there was wonder on the stepmother.

The next day when he drove out the cows the stepmother told the second daughter to follow him, and to be watching him till she would see where he was getting things to eat. The daughter followed him and put herself in hiding, but when the heat of the day came the music began and she fell asleep. The lad took the horn off the bull, drew out the tablecloth, the food and drink, ate and drank his enough, and put back the horn again. The girl woke then, and was watching him until the evening. When the evening came he drove the cows home, and he was not able to eat his supper any more than the two evenings before. The stepmother asked the daughter did she see anything, and she said she did not. There was wonder on the stepmother.

The next day, when the lad went out herding cows, the stepmother sent the third daughter out after him, and threatened her not to fall asleep, but to have a good watch. The daughter followed the lad, and went into hiding. This daughter had three eyes, for she had an eye in the back of her head. When the bracket bull began playing every music more excellent than another he put the other eyes to sleep, but he was not able to put the third eye to sleep. When the heat of the day came she saw the bracket bull coming to the boy, and the boy taking the horn off him and eating.

She ran home then and said to her mother that there wasn't such a dinner in the world as was being set before the boy out of the horn of the bracket bull.

Then the mother let on that she was sick, and she killed a cock, and she let down its blood into her bed, and she put up a sup of the blood into her mouth, and she sent for her husband saying that she was finding death [dying]. Her husband came in and he saw the blood, and he said: 'Anything that is in the world that would save her that she must get it.' She said that there wasn't a thing in the world that would save her but a piece of the bracket bull that was on the mountain.

'You must get that,' said he.

The bracket bull used to be the first one of the cattle that used to come in every night, and the stepmother sent for two butchers, and she set them on each side of the gate to kill the bracket bull when he would come.

The bracket bull said to the boy, 'I'll be swept [done for] to-night, unless another cow goes before me.' He put another cow out before him and the two butchers were standing on each side of the gate to kill the first one that would come in. The bull sent the cow out before him, going through the gate, and they killed her: and then the stepmother got a piece of her to eat, and she thought it was the bracket bull that she was eating, and she got better then.

The next night, when the lad came home with the cattle, he ate no more of his supper than any other night, and there was wonder on the stepmother. She heard after this that the bracket bull was in it all through, and that he was not killed at that time.

When she heard that she killed a cock, and she let down some of its blood into her bed, and she put a sup of the blood into her mouth, and she played the same trick over again, and said that there was nothing at all to cure her but a piece of the bracket bull.

The butchers were sent for, and they were ready to kill the bracket bull as soon as he came in. The bracket bull sent another one of the cattle in before himself, and the butchers killed it. The woman got part of its flesh, and she thought that it was part of the bracket bull she was eating and she got better.

She found out afterwards that it was not the bracket bull that was dead, and she said, 'Never mind! I'll kill the bracket bull yet!'

The next day when the lad was herding the cows on the mountain the bracket bull came and said to him – 'Take the horn off me and eat your enough now. That's the last time for you. They are waiting to kill me to-night but don't you be afraid. It is not they who shall kill me, but another bull shall kill me. Get up on my back now.'

The lad got up on his back then and they went home. The two butchers were on each side of the gate waiting for him. The bracket bull stuck a horn on each side of him, and he killed the two butchers. Out with him then, and the lad on his back.

He went into a wild wood, and he himself and the lad spent the night in that wood. He was to fight with the other bull on the next day.

When the day came the bracket bull said, 'Take the horn off me and eat your enough – that's the last luck you have. I am to fight with the other bull immediately, and I shall escape from him to-day, but he will have me dead to-morrow by twelve o'clock.'

Himself and the other bull fought that day, and the bracket bull came back in the evening and he himself and the lad passed that night in the wood.

When the next day came the bracket bull said to him – 'Twist the horn off me and eat your enough, that's the last luck you'll have. Listen now to the thing that I'm telling you. When you'll see me dead go and cut a strip of skin of the back and a strip of the stomach off me, and make a belt of it, and any time at all there will be any hard pinch on you, you shall have my power.'

The bracket bull went then to fight with the other bull, and the other bull killed him. The other bull went away then. The lad came to the bracket bull where he was lying on the ground, and he was not dead out-and-out. When he saw the boy coming he said – 'Oh,' said he, 'make haste as well as you can in the world, and take out your knife and cut that strip off me or you will be killed as well as myself.'

There was a trembling in the poor creature's hand and he was not able to cut a piece at all off the bull, after his feeding him for so long, and after the kindness he had got from him.

The bracket bull spoke again and told him to cut the strip off him on the instant and that it would assist him as long as he would be alive. He cut a strip off the back then and another strip off the belly, and he went away.

There was plenty of trouble and of grief on him, going of him, and he ought to have that on him too, and he departing without any knowledge of where he was making for, or where he would go.

A gentleman met him on the road and asked him where he was going. The lad said that he did not himself know where he was going, but that he was going looking for work.

'What are you able to do?' says the gentleman.

'I'm as good a herd as ever you saw, but I'll not tell you a lie, I can do nothing but herding; but indeed I'll do that as well as any man that ever you saw.'

'It's you I want,' says the gentleman. 'There are three giants up by my land, on the one mearing with me, and anything that will go in on their land they will keep it, and I cannot take it of them again. That's all they're asking – my cattle to go in across the mearing to them.'

'Never mind them. I'll go bail that I'll take good heed of them, and that I'll not let anything in to them.'

The gentleman brought him home then, and he went herding for him. When the grass was getting scarce he was driving the cows further out. There was a big stone wall between the land of the giants and his master's land. There was fine grass on the other side of the wall. When he saw that, he threw down a gap in the wall and let in the pigs and the cows. He went up into a tree then and was throwing down apples and all sorts [of fruit] to the pigs.

A giant came out, and when he saw the lad up on the tree throwing down the apples to the pigs, the bead rose on him [*i.e.* he got furious]. He came to the tree. 'Get down out of that,' says he. 'I think you big for one bite and small for two bites; come down till I draw you under my long cold teeth.'

'Arrah, take yourself easy,' says the boy; 'perhaps it's too quick I'd come down to you.'

'I won't be talking to you any longer,' says the giant; he got a leverage on the tree and drew it up out of the roots.

'Go down, black thong, and squeeze that fellow,' says the lad, for he remembered the advice of the bracket bull. On the instant the black thong leaped out of his hand, and squeezed the giant so hard that the two eyes were going out on his head, for stronger was the power of the bull than the power of the giant. The giant was not able to put a stir out of himself, and he promised anything at all – only to save his life for him. 'Anything at all you want,' says he to the lad, 'you must get it from me.'

'I'm not asking anything at all except the loan of the sword that's under your bed,' says he.

'I give it to you, and welcome,' says the giant. He went in, and brought out the sword with him.

'Try it on the three biggest trees that are in the wood, and you won't feel it in your hand going through them,' says the giant.

'I don't see any tree in the wood bigger or uglier than yourself,' says he, drawing the sword and whipping the head off him, so that he sent it seven furrows and seven ridges with that stroke.

'If I were to get on the body again,' said the head, and it talking, 'and the men of the world wouldn't get me off the trunk again.'

'I'll take good care, myself, of that,' says the lad.

When he drove the cows home in the evening they had that much milk that they had not half enough of vessels, and two coopers were obliged to make new vessels to hold the quantity of milk they had.

'You're the best lad that ever I met,' says the gentleman and he was thankful to him.

The giants used to put – each man of them – a shout out of him every evening. The people only heard two shouts that evening. 'There's some change in the caher tonight,' said the gentleman, when he heard the two shouts.

'Oh,' says the lad, 'I saw one of them going away by himself to-day and he did not come home yet.'

On the next day the lad drove out his cattle until he came to the big stone wall, and he threw a gap in it, and let the cattle into the same place. He went up into a tree and began throwing down the apples. The second giant came running and said, 'What's the meaning of throwing my wall and letting in your cattle on my estate? Get down out of that at once. You killed my brother yesterday.'

'Go down, black thong and bind that one,' says the lad. The thong squeezed him so that he was not able to put a stir out of himself, and he promised the lad anything at all – only to spare his life.

'I am asking nothing of you but the loan of the old sword that is under your bed.'

'I'll give you that and welcome.' He went in and brought out the sword with him. Each man of them had a sword, and every sword better than another.

'Try that sword on the six biggest trees that are in the wood, and it will go through them without turning the edge.'

'I don't see any tree in the wood bigger or uglier than yourself,' says he, drawing the sword and whipping the head off him, so that he sent it seven furrows and seven ridges from the body.

'Oh,' said the head, 'if I were to get going on the body again and the men of the world wouldn't get me off it again.'

'Oh, I'll take care of that myself,' says the boy.

When he drove the cows home that night there was wonder on the people when they saw the quantity of milk they had. The gentleman said that there was another change in the caher that day again, as he did not hear but only one shout, but the lad said that he saw another one going away that day, and that it was likely that he did not come back yet.

On the next day he went out, and drove the pigs and the cows up to the hall-door, and was throwing down the apples to them. The third giant came out – the eldest man of them – and he was full mad after his two brothers being dead, and the teeth that were in his head were making a hand-stick for him. He told the boy to come down; that he did not know what he would do to him after his having killed his two brothers. 'Come down,' says he, 'till I draw you under my long, cold teeth,' and it was on him the long, cold teeth were, and no lie.

'Go down, black thong, and bind that one till the eyes will be going out on his head with the power of the squeezing that you'll give him.'

The black thong leaped from him, and it bound the giant until the two eyes were going out on his head with the squeezing and with the tightening it gave him, and the giant promised to give him anything at all, 'but spare my life,' says he.

'I'm only asking the loan of the old sword that's under your bed,' said the lad.

'Have it, and welcome,' says the giant. He went in and brought out the sword with him. 'Now,' says the giant, 'strike the two ugliest stumps in the wood and the sword will cut them without getting a bent edge.'

'Musha, then, by Mary,' says the boy, 'I don't see any stump in the wood uglier than yourself,' and he struck him so that he sent his head seven furrows and seven ridges from the body.

'Ochone for ever!' says the head, 'if I were to get going on the body again, the men of the world – they wouldn't get me off the body again.'

'I'll take care of that myself,' says the boy.

When he came home that night the coopers were not able to make enough of vessels for them to hold the quantity of milk that the cows had, and the pigs were not able to eat with the quantity of apples that they had eaten before that.

He was a while in that way herding the cows and everything that was in the castle, he had it. There was not one at all going near the castle, for there was fear on them.

There was a fiery dragon in that country and he used to come every seven years, and unless there would be a young woman ready bound before him he would drive the sea through the land, and he would destroy the people. The day came when the dragon was to come, and the lad asked his master to let him go to the place where the dragon was coming. 'What's the business you have there?' says the master, 'there will be horsemen and coaches and great people there, and the crowds will be gathered together in it out of every place. The horses would rise up on top of you, and you would be crushed under their feet; and it's better for you to stop at home.'

'I'll stop,' said the lad. But when he got them all gone he went to the castle of the three giants, and he put a saddle on the best steed they had, and a fine suit on himself, and he took the first giant's sword in his hand, and he went to where the dragon was.

It was like a fair there, with the number of riders and coaches and horses and people that were gathered in it. There was a young lady bound to a post on the brink of the sea, and she waiting for the dragon to come to swallow her. It was the King's daughter that was in it, for the dragon would not take any other woman. When the dragon came out of the sea the lad went against him, and they fought with one another, and were fighting till the evening, until the dragon was frothing at the mouth, and till the sea was red with its blood. He turned the dragon out into the sea at last. He went away then, and said that he would return the next day. He left the steed again in the place where he found it, and he took the fine suit off him, and when the other people returned he was before them. When the people came home that night they were all talking and saying that some champion came to fight with the dragon and turned him out into the sea again. That was the story that every person had, but they did not know who was the champion who did it.

The next day when his master and the other people were gone, he went to the castle of the three giants again and he took out another steed and another suit of valour [*i.e.* armour] and he brought with him the second giant's sword, and he went to the place where the dragon was to come.

The King's daughter was bound to a post on the shore, waiting for him, and the eyes going out on her head looking would she see the champion coming who fought the dragon the day before. There were twice as many people in it as there were on the other day, and they were all waiting till they would see the champion coming. When the dragon came the lad went in face of him, and the dragon was half confused and sickened after the fight that he had made the day before. They were beating one another till the evening, and then he drove away the dragon. The people tried to keep him, but they were not able. He went from them.

When his master came home that evening the lad was in the house before him. The master told him that another champion came that day, and that he had turned the dragon into the sea. But no doubt the lad knew the story better himself than he did.

On the next day, when the gentleman was gone, he went to the caher of the giants and he took with him another steed and another suit and the sword of the third giant, and when he came to fight with the dragon the people thought it was another champion who was in it.

He himself and the dragon were beating each other then, and the sorra such a fight you ever saw. There were wings on the dragon, and when he was getting it tight he rose up in the air, and he was thrusting and beating the boy in his skull till he was nearly destroyed. He remembered the black thong then and said, 'Black thong, bind that one so hard that they'll be listening to his screeching in the two divisions of the world with the squeezing that you'll give him.' The black thong leapt away and she bound him, and then the lad took the head off him, and the sea was red with his blood, and the waves of blood were going on the top of the water.

The lad came to the land then, and they tried to keep him; but he went from them, and as he was riding by the lady snatched the shoe off him.

He went away then, and he left the horse and the sword and the suit of armour in the place where he found them, and when the gentleman and the other people came home he was sitting before them at the fire. He asked them how the fight went, and they told him that the champion killed the fiery dragon, but that he was gone away, and that no one at all knew who he was.

When the King's daughter came home she said that she would never marry a man but the man whom that shoe would fit.

There were sons of kings, and great people among them, and they saying that it was themselves who killed the dragon, but she said it was not they, unless the shoe would fit them. Some of them were cutting the toes off their feet, and some of them taking off a piece of the heel, and more of them cutting the big toe off themselves, trying would the shoe fit them. There was no good for them in it. The King's daughter said that she would not marry one man of them.

She sent out soldiers then, and the shoe with them, to try would it fit anyone at all. Every person, poor and rich, no matter where he was from, must try the shoe on him.

The lad was stretched out lying on the grass when the soldiers came, and when they saw him they said to him, 'Shoe your foot.'

'Oh, don't be humbugging me,' says he.

'We have orders,' said they, 'and we cannot return without trying the shoe on everyone, poor and rich, so stretch out your foot.' He did that, and the shoe went on his foot on the moment.

They said to him that he must come with them.

'Oh, listen to me' [*i.e.* give me time], said he, 'till I dress myself.'

He went to the caher of the giants, and he got a fine new suit on him, and he went with them then.

That's where the welcome was for him, and he as dressed up as e'er a man of them. They had a wedding for three days and three nights.

They got the pond and I the lakelet. They were drowned, and I came [through]. And as I have it [*i.e.* the story] to-night, that ye may not have it to-morrow night, or if ye have it, itself, that ye may only lose the back teeth by it!

Fair, Brown, and Trembling

Source: Jeremiah Curtin, *Myths and Folk-Lore of Ireland*, London, Sampson Low, Marston, Searle, & Rivington, 1890.

This story, translated by the American Jeremiah Curtin from the Gaelic, was, he writes, 'collected by me personally in the West of Ireland . . . during the year 1887'. The contest between suitors is unusual; the continuation after the wedding, with its story of the substituted bride along the lines of the widely distributed tale known as 'The Black and the White Bride' (AT403), is less so, but it still has some striking features – especially the whale which three times swallows and casts out the heroine. In many similar stories the true bride is actually transformed into an animal after being thrown into water.

I have altered Curtin's 'cowboy' to 'cowherd' to avoid unfortunate associations. 'Omanya' is the ancient kingdom of Emania in Ulster.

KING AEDH CÚRUCHA lived in Tir Conal, and he had three daughters, whose names were Fair, Brown, and Trembling.

Fair and Brown had new dresses, and went to church every Sunday. Trembling was kept at home to do the cooking and work. They would not let her go out of the house at all; for she was more beautiful than the other two, and they were in dread she might marry before themselves.

They carried on in this way for seven years. At the end of seven years the son of the king of Omanya fell in love with the eldest sister.

One Sunday morning, after the other two had gone to church, the old henwife came into the kitchen to Trembling, and said: 'It's at church you ought to be this day, instead of working here at home.'

'How could I go?' said Trembling. 'I have no clothes good enough to wear at church; and if my sisters were to see me there, they'd kill me for going out of the house.'

'I'll give you,' said the henwife, 'a finer dress than either of them has ever seen. And now tell me what dress will you have?'

'I'll have,' said Trembling, 'a dress as white as snow, and green shoes for my feet.'

Then the henwife put on the cloak of darkness, clipped a piece from the old clothes the young woman had on, and asked for the whitest robes in the world and the most beautiful that could be found, and a pair of green shoes.

That moment she had the robe and the shoes, and she brought them to Trembling, who put them on. When Trembling was dressed and ready, the henwife said: 'I have a honey-bird here to sit on your right shoulder, and a honey-finger to put on your left. At the door stands a milk-white mare, with a golden saddle for you to sit on, and a golden bridle to hold in your hand.'

Trembling sat on the golden saddle; and when she was ready to start, the henwife said: 'You must not go inside the door of the church, and the minute the people rise up at the end of Mass, do you make off, and ride home as fast as the mare will carry you.'

When Trembling came to the door of the church there was no one inside who could get a glimpse of her but was striving to know who she was; and when they saw her hurrying away at the end of Mass, they ran out to overtake her. But no use in their running; she was away before any man could come near her. From the minute she left the church till she got home, she overtook the wind before her, and outstripped the wind behind.

She came down at the door, went in, and found the henwife had dinner ready. She put off the white robes, and had on her old dress in a twinkling.

When the two sisters came home the henwife asked: 'Have you any news to-day from the church?'

'We have great news,' said they. 'We saw a wonderful, grand lady at the church-door. The like of the robes she had we have never seen on woman before. It's little that was thought of our dresses beside what she had on; and there wasn't a man at the church, from the king to the beggar, but was trying to look at her and know who she was.'

The sisters would give no peace till they had two dresses like the robes of the strange lady; but honey-birds and honey-fingers were not to be found.

Next Sunday the two sisters went to church again, and left the youngest at home to cook the dinner.

After they had gone, the henwife came in and asked: 'Will you go to church to-day?'

'I would go,' said Trembling, 'if I could get the going.'

'What robe will you wear?' asked the henwife.

'The finest black satin that can be found, and red shoes for my feet.'

'What color do you want the mare to be?'

'I want her to be so black and so glossy that I can see myself in her body.'

The henwife put on the cloak of darkness, and asked for the robes and the mare. That moment she had them. When Trembling was dressed, the henwife put the honey-bird on her right shoulder and the honey-finger on her left. The saddle on the mare was silver, and so was the bridle.

When Trembling sat in the saddle and was going away, the henwife ordered her strictly not to go inside the door of the church, but to rush away as soon as the people rose at the end of Mass, and hurry home on the mare before any man could stop her.

That Sunday the people were more astonished than ever, and gazed at her more than the first time; and all they were thinking of was to know who she was. But they had no chance; for the moment the people rose at the end of Mass she slipped from the church, was in the silver saddle, and home before a man could stop her or talk to her.

The henwife had the dinner ready. Trembling took off her satin robe, and had on her old clothes before her sisters got home.

'What news have you to-day?' asked the henwife of the sisters when they came from the church.

'Oh, we saw the grand strange lady again! And it's little that any man could think of our dresses after looking at the robes of satin that she had on! And all at church, from high to low, had their mouths open, gazing at her, and no man was looking at us.'

The two sisters gave neither rest nor peace till they got dresses as nearly like the strange lady's robes as they could find. Of course they were not so good; for the like of those robes could not be found in Erin.

When the third Sunday came, Fair and Brown went to church dressed in black satin. They left Trembling at home to work in the kitchen, and told her to be sure and have dinner ready when they came back.

After they had gone and were out of sight, the henwife came to the kitchen and said: 'Well, my dear, are you for church to-day?'

'I would go if I had a new dress to wear.'

'I'll get you any dress you ask for. What dress would you like?' asked the henwife.

'A dress red as a rose from the waist down, and white as snow from the waist up; a cape of green on my shoulders; and a hat on my head with a red, a white, and a green feather in it; and shoes for my feet with the toes red, the middle white, and the backs and heels green.'

The henwife put on the cloak of darkness, wished for all these things, and had them. When Trembling was dressed, the henwife put the honey-bird on her right shoulder and the honey-finger on her left, and placing the hat on her head, clipped a few hairs from one lock and a few from another with her scissors, and that moment the most beautiful golden hair was flowing down over the girl's shoulders. Then the henwife asked what kind of a mare she would ride. She said white, with blue and gold-colored diamond-shaped spots all over her body, on her back a saddle of gold, and on her head a golden bridle.

The mare stood there before the door, and a bird sitting between her ears, which began to sing as soon as Trembling was in the saddle, and never stopped till she came home from the church.

The fame of the beautiful strange lady had gone out through the world, and all the princes and great men that were in it came to church that Sunday, each one hoping that it was himself would have her home with him after Mass.

The son of the king of Omanya forgot all about the eldest sister, and remained outside the church, so as to catch the strange lady before she could hurry away.

The church was more crowded than ever before, and there were three times as many outside. There was such a throng before the church that Trembling could only come inside the gate.

As soon as the people were rising at the end of Mass, the lady slipped out through the gate, was in the golden saddle in an instant, and sweeping away ahead of the wind. But if she was, the prince of Omanya was at her side, and, seizing her by the foot, he ran with the mare for thirty perches, and never let go of the beautiful lady till the shoe was pulled from her foot, and he was left behind with it in his hand. She came home as fast as the mare could carry her, and was thinking all the time that the henwife would kill her for losing the shoe.

Seeing her so vexed and so changed in the face, the old woman asked: 'What's the trouble that's on you now?'

'Oh! I've lost one of the shoes off my feet,' said Trembling.

'Don't mind that; don't be vexed,' said the henwife; 'maybe it's the best thing that ever happened to you.'

Then Trembling gave up all the things she had to the henwife, put on her old clothes, and went to work in the kitchen. When the sisters came home, the henwife asked: 'Have you any news from the church?'

'We have indeed,' said they; 'for we saw the grandest sight to-day. The strange lady came again, in grander array than before. On herself and the horse she rode were the finest colors of the world, and between the ears of the horse was a bird which never stopped singing from the time she came till she went away. The lady herself is the most beautiful woman ever seen by man in Erin.'

After Trembling had disappeared from the church, the son of the king of Omanya said to the other kings' sons: 'I will have that lady for my own.'

They all said: 'You didn't win her just by taking the shoe off her foot, you'll have to win her by the point of the sword; you'll have to fight for her with us before you can call her your own.'

'Well,' said the son of the king of Omanya, 'when I find the lady that shoe will fit, I'll fight for her, never fear, before I leave her to any of you.'

Then all the kings' sons were uneasy, and anxious to know who was she that lost the shoe; and they began to travel all over Erin to know could they find her. The prince of Omanya and all the others went in a great company together, and made the round of Erin; they went every-where – north, south, east, and west. They visited every place where a woman was to be found, and left not a house in the kingdom they did not search, to know could they find the woman the shoe would fit, not caring whether she was rich or poor, of high or low degree.

The prince of Omanya always kept the shoe; and when the young women saw it, they had great hopes, for it was of proper size, neither large nor small, and it would beat any man to know of what material it was made. One thought it would fit her if she cut a little from her great toe; and another, with too short a foot, put something in the tip of her stocking. But no use, they only spoiled their feet, and were curing them for months afterwards.

The two sisters, Fair and Brown, heard that the princes of the world were looking all over Erin for the woman that could wear the shoe, and every day they were talking of trying it on; and one day Trembling spoke up and said: 'Maybe it's my foot that the shoe will fit.'

'Oh, the breaking of the dog's foot on you! Why say so when you were at home every Sunday?'

They were that way waiting, and scolding the younger sister, till the princes were near the place. The day they were to come, the sisters put Trembling in a closet, and locked the door on her. When the company came to the house, the prince of Omanya gave the shoe to the sisters. But though they tried and tried, it would fit neither of them.

'Is there any other young woman in the house?' asked the prince.

'There is,' said Trembling, speaking up in the closet; 'I'm here.'

'Oh! we have her for nothing but to put out the ashes,' said the sisters.

But the prince and the others wouldn't leave the house till they had seen her; so the two sisters had to open the door. When Trembling came out, the shoe was given to her, and it fitted exactly.

The prince of Omanya looked at her and said: 'You are the woman the shoe fits, and you are the woman I took the shoe from.'

Then Trembling spoke up, and said: 'Do you stay here till I return.'

Then she went to the henwife's house. The old woman put on the cloak of darkness, got everything for her she had the first Sunday at church, and put her on the white mare in the same fashion. Then Trembling rode along the highway to the front of the house. All who saw her the first time said: 'This is the lady we saw at church.'

Then she went away a second time, and a second time she came back on the black mare in the second dress which the henwife gave her. All who saw her the second Sunday said: 'That is the lady we saw at church.'

A third time she asked for a short absence, and soon came back on the third mare and in the third dress. All who saw her the third time said: 'That is the lady we saw at church.' Every man was satisfied, and knew that she was the woman.

Then all the princes and great men spoke up, and said to the son of the king of Omanya: 'You'll have to fight now for her before we let her go with you.'

'I'm here before you, ready for combat,' answered the prince.

Then the son of the king of Lochlin stepped forth. The struggle began, and a terrible struggle it was. They fought for nine hours; and then the son of the king of Lochlin stopped, gave up his claim, and left

the field. Next day the son of the king of Spain fought six hours, and
yielded his claim. On the third day the son of the king of Nyerfói
fought eight hours, and stopped. The fourth day the son of the king of
Greece fought six hours, and stopped. On the fifth day no more
strange princes wanted to fight; and all the sons of kings in Erin said
they would not fight with a man of their own land, that the strangers
had had their chance, and as no others came to claim the woman, she
belonged of right to the son of the king of Omanya.

The marriage-day was fixed, and the invitations were sent out. The
wedding lasted for a year and a day. When the wedding was over, the
king's son brought home the bride, and when the time came a son was
born. The young woman sent for her eldest sister, Fair, to be with her
and care for her. One day, when Trembling was well, and when her
husband was away hunting, the two sisters went out to walk; and
when they came to the seaside, the eldest pushed the youngest sister in.
A great whale came and swallowed her.

The eldest sister came home alone, and the husband asked, 'Where is
your sister?'

'She has gone home to her father in Ballyshannon; now that I am
well, I don't need her.'

'Well,' said the husband, looking at her, 'I'm in dread it's my wife
that has gone.'

'Oh! no,' said she; 'it's my sister Fair that's gone.'

Since the sisters were very much alike, the prince was in doubt. That
night he put his sword between them, and said: 'If you are my wife,
this sword will get warm; if not, it will stay cold.'

In the morning when he rose up, the sword was as cold as when he
put it there.

It happened when the two sisters were walking by the seashore, that
a little cowherd was down by the water minding cattle, and saw Fair
push Trembling into the sea; and next day, when the tide came in, he
saw the whale swim up and throw her out on the sand. When she was
on the sand she said to the cowherd: 'When you go home in the
evening with the cows, tell the master that my sister Fair pushed me
into the sea yesterday; that a whale swallowed me, and then threw me
out, but will come again and swallow me with the coming of the next
tide; then he'll go out with the tide, and come again with to-morrow's
tide, and throw me again on the strand. The whale will cast me out
three times. I'm under the enchantment of this whale, and cannot leave
the beach or escape myself. Unless my husband saves me before I'm

swallowed the fourth time, I shall be lost. He must come and shoot the whale with a silver bullet when he turns on the broad of his back. Under the breast-fin of the whale is a reddish-brown spot. My husband must hit him in that spot, for it is the only place in which he can be killed.'

When the cowherd got home, the eldest sister gave him a draught of oblivion, and he did not tell.

Next day he went again to the sea. The whale came and cast Trembling on shore again. She asked the boy: 'Did you tell the master what I told you to tell him?'

'I did not,' said he; 'I forgot.'

'How did you forget?' asked she.

'The woman of the house gave me a drink that made me forget.'

'Well, don't forget telling him this night; and if she gives you a drink, don't take it from her.'

As soon as the cowherd came home, the eldest sister offered him a drink. He refused to take it till he had delivered his message and told all to the master. The third day the prince went down with his gun and a silver bullet in it. He was not long down when the whale came and threw Trembling upon the beach as the two days before. She had no power to speak to her husband till he had killed the whale. Then the whale went out, turned over once on the broad of his back, and showed the spot for a moment only. That moment the prince fired. He had but the one chance, and a short one at that; but he took it, and hit the spot, and the whale, mad with pain, made the sea all around red with blood, and died.

That minute Trembling was able to speak, and went home with her husband, who sent word to her father what the eldest sister had done. The father came, and told him any death he chose to give her to give it. The prince told the father he would leave her life and death with himself. The father had her put out then on the sea in a barrel, with provisions in it for seven years.

In time Trembling had a second child, a daughter. The prince and she sent the cowherd to school, and trained him up as one of their own children, and said: 'If the little girl that is born to us now lives, no other man in the world will get her but him.'

The cowherd and the prince's daughter lived on till they were married. The mother said to her husband: 'You could not have saved me from the whale but for the little cowherd; on that account I don't grudge him my daughter.'

The son of the king of Omanya and Trembling had fourteen children, and they lived happily till the two died of old age.

Maria

Source: Fletcher Gardner, 'Filipino (Tagalog) Versions of Cinderella', *Journal of American Folk-lore*, vol. XIX, New York, The American Folk-lore Society, October–December 1906.

Fletcher Gardner collected this story in December 1903 at Mangarin, Mindoro, from a young man called Cornelio, who had heard it from a man from Marinduque Island. Gardner writes, 'The story was taken down by my usual method of listening attentively to the tale in Tagalog, and then at once writing it out in English, from memory, and having this story retold, with the translation at hand, to detect inaccuracies.' It is very similar to Gardner's second text, collected from a woman of about sixty at Pola, Mindoro, in October of the same year.

In a 'comparative note' attached to Gardner's translations, William Wells Newell asserts that the Cinderella story must have travelled to the Philippines via Spanish, and translates a Chilean Spanish version, 'Maria the Ash-Girl', which is roughly equivalent to the first half of the Tagalog story. In it, the stepsister receives 'the wattles of a turkey gobbler' on her forehead, rather than a bell. The continuation, in which Maria's children are stolen and substituted with puppies, is also of European origin, and can be found in many folktales and medieval romances. It is familiar from Chaucer's 'Man of Law's Tale'. The two tale types in which this motif of the calumniated wife is most frequently found are 'The Maiden without Hands' (AT706) and 'The Three Golden Sons' (AT707).

Other Cinderellas from the Philippines can be found in Dean S. Fansler, 'Metrical Romances in the Philippines', and in Fansler's *Filipino Popular Tales*. The romance of 'The Life of Maria' summarized by Fansler is evidently the source for both Gardner's Tagalog versions.

Don V. Hart and Harriet C. Hart give a valuable summary of the Philippine folktale in their essay 'Cinderella in the Eastern Bisayas' (*Journal of American Folklore*, 79, 1966), in which they print three Cinderella versions collected in eastern Samar. These do not proceed beyond the marriage. In one of them, 'The Girl with a Star on her Forehead', narrated by a sixty-five-year-old spinster, Maria, who heard the story from her mother, the second girl's disfigurement is more potent and suggestive than either a bell or a turkey comb. The unnamed Cinderella figure is maid-of-all-work in her aunt's house. The aunt is cruel to her, beats her, and orders her to wash white clothes black, and black clothes white. This she achieves, with the help of an old woman. Then the aunt kills and eats the girl's chicken. The old woman tells the girl to save the feathers, and the feathers grow into a big house. But the girl remains with her cruel aunt. When she is exhausted with work, the old woman combs her hair; when she touches the girl's forehead, a star appears there, and when she touches her stomach, a moon appears. The aunt and her daughter go to church, leaving the girl to do a mountain of work before following. The old woman does the work, and tells the girl to jump in a well. When she does so, she is swallowed by a fish, which vomits her out, dressed in finery. She goes to church to find Mass already over. The old woman tells her to leave a slipper by the door. The king finds the shoe, and marries the girl, and they live in the house made from the chicken feathers. The aunt visits them, and asks how all this good fortune has come about. The end is worth giving in full:

> The aunt went home, thinking that if she were cruel to her own daughter her child would become like the niece – have a big house and marry a prince.
>
> So she ordered her daughter to do all the household tasks. She beat her just as she had the niece. But the daughter always spoke badly to her mother, saying she was crazy. Even when the daughter obeyed, the mother would beat her.
>
> One day she told her daughter to wash the clothes and to make the black clothes white and the white ones black. Immediately she beat her. The girl flung bad words at her mother. The more she spoke badly the angrier the mother became. But the daughter was obliged to do the washing. When she got to the place where she was to do the wash, she felt sleepy and went to sleep.
>
> When she awoke her clothes were missing. She could not see

them. She became very angry. The same old woman appeared and asked her, 'Why are you angry?'

'Perhaps you are the one who stole my clothes,' the girl answered angrily. 'Return them to me!'

'Come with me, and I'll return your clothes,' said the old woman.

She returned the washed clothes and the black ones had been changed to white and the white ones to black. The old woman then touched the girl's forehead and immediately a vagina appeared, without the girl's knowledge. She then touched her stomach and a penis appeared, but the girl did not notice it either. When the daughter returned home her mother beat her. Again the daughter called her mother bad words. After the mother had been beating her for a long time she saw the vagina and penis on her body. She was so ashamed that she locked her daughter in a room so no one could see her.

People who knew that this woman had a daughter came to ask for her hand in marriage. One day the first visitor was in the house, but the daughter was locked in the room. The girl was eager to see the man who was courting her. So she climbed the wall to see the man. But when she got to the top she felt sleepy. She fell into the room where the young man and her mother were sitting. She urinated very much. All the people ran away from her. She was never able to marry.

One function of traditional stories is as a source of social control; here, the first girl's passive obedience and acceptance of cruel treatment leads to riches and a happy marriage; the second girl's more spirited response brings physical degradation and humiliation, and prevents her ever marrying.

ONCE THERE WERE a man and his wife who had a daughter named Maria. Maria was a very pretty child and very happy, but unfortunately her father fell in love with a woman who was not his wife, and one day taking his wife out to fish with him he murdered her and threw her body into the water. Poor little Maria cried a great deal after her mother's death, but her lot was worse after her father married the other woman, for the stepmother set her all kinds of cruel tasks and threatened her with awful penalties if she failed.

Maria had a pet pig, with which she played a great deal, and her stepmother ordered her to kill and clean it. Poor little Maria cried and begged, but the woman forced her to kill the pig. When the pig was cleaned, the stepmother gave Maria ten of the refuse pieces and told

her to clean them in the river, and if one piece was missing when she returned, she would be beaten to death. Maria cleaned the pieces in the river, but one slipped away and went down stream. The child cried and lamented over her fate so that an old crocodile going by asked her what was amiss. 'That is nothing,' said the crocodile, and he straightway swam after the piece and brought it back. As he turned to swim away, he splashed with his tail and a drop of water fell on her forehead where it became a most beautiful jewel, flashing like the sun and fastened so tightly that it could not be removed. The little girl went home with the jewel on her forehead shining so brightly that it made every one cross-eyed to look at it, so that it had to be covered with a handkerchief.

The cruel stepmother asked many questions about Maria's good fortune, and when she found out all about it she sent her own daughter to kill a pig and do in all respects as the stepsister had done.

She did so and threw a piece of refuse meat into the river and cried as it floated off.

The crocodile inquired of this girl also the cause of the trouble, and again brought the meat, but this time when he splashed with his tail, instead of a jewel on the girl's forehead, there was a little bell that tinkled incessantly. All the people knelt and crossed themselves because they thought the 'Viaticum' passed, but when they saw the bell on the girl's forehead they laughed and pointed at her. So the daughter had to tie up her forehead for shame, for the bell could not be gotten off.

The stepmother was more cruel than ever to Maria now that she had met with good fortune and her daughter with ill. She set the girl to every kind of dirty work till her whole body was filthy and then sent her to the river to bathe, telling her that if she did not wash her back clean she would beat her to death.

Maria struggled and scrubbed, but she could not reach her back either to see whether it was clean or to wash it, and she began to cry. Out of the river came a great she-crab, that asked the girl her trouble. 'Oh,' said Maria, 'if I do not wash my back clean my stepmother will beat me to death.' 'Very well,' said the crab, 'that is easily remedied,' and jumping on to Maria's back scrubbed and scrubbed till her back was perfectly clean. 'Now,' said the crab, 'you must eat me and take my shell home and bury it in the yard. Something will grow up that will be valuable to you.' Maria did as she was told, and from the place grew a fine lukban (grapefruit) tree which in time bore fruit.

One day the stepmother and her daughter wished to go to church and left Maria to get the dinner. The stepmother told her that dinner must be ready when she returned and must be neither cold nor hot. Maria wept again over the impossibility of the task and was about to despair when an old woman came in, to whom she told her troubles. The old woman was a stranger but was apparently very wise, for she told Maria to go to church and that she would prepare the dinner. The girl said she had no clothes, but the old woman told her to look in the fruit of the lukban tree, and from the fruit Maria took out all the garments of a princess, a beautiful chariot and eight horses. Quickly she bathed and arrayed herself and drove by the king's palace to the church, the jewel on her forehead shining so that it nearly blinded all who looked. The king, seeing such a magnificently dressed princess, sent his soldiers to find out about her, but they could learn nothing and had nothing to show when they returned but one of her little slippers which fell off as she left the church.

Maria went home and hastily put the dress and equipage back into the lukban fruit, and the old woman was there waiting with the dinner, which was neither cold nor hot. When the stepmother came from church, she saw only her stepdaughter there in rags, and everything ready according to her order.

Now the king wished to know who this princess was and ordered a 'bando' sent around to every woman and girl in the kingdom, saying he would marry whomever the shoe would fit. The stepmother and her daughter went to the palace, but tied Maria in a sack and set her in the fireplace, telling her that she would be beaten to death if she stirred. The shoe fitted nobody at the palace; whether their feet were long, short, broad, narrow, big, little, or otherwise, it fitted no one. So the soldiers were sent out again to bring in every one who had not obeyed the 'bando' and they looked into the house where Maria lived, but they did not see her. Just then a cock crowed and said, 'Kikiriki, that's the girl. Kikiriki, there in the fireplace; the shoe fits her foot.' So the soldiers made Maria dress in her finery with the mate to her little slipper on her foot, and with her little chariot and the eight ponies she went to the king's palace, and the other little slipper fitted exactly.

The stepmother and her daughter were envious, but could do nothing against the king's wishes, and the king married Maria with great pomp, but none of the jewels were so beautiful as the one that blazed on Maria's forehead.

In due time it came to be known that an heir would be born, but the king was called away to war. He arranged that a signal should be set, however, – a white flag if all went well and a black flag if anything went wrong.

He left the princess in the care of her stepmother and two wise women, and warned them not to let anything bad happen to the queen. The stepmother had not forgotten her hate for Maria, and when the little princes were born, for there were seven, she and the other women took them away and substituted seven little blind puppies.

When the king returned he saw the black flag flying over the tower and hurried to the queen's rooms to find her in tears over the puppies. He ordered the puppies drowned and his wife put into a corner under the staircase, until a place could be built for her. Then he had a hut built outside the palace and placed the queen there in chains.

The seven little princes, stolen from their mother, were put into a box which was cast into the sea and which drifted far away to a shore near an enchanter's cave. This enchanter had an oracle which spoke to him and said, 'Go by the mountains and you will be sad, go by the shore and you will be glad,' as he was setting out for his daily walk. Obedient to the oracle, he went to the shore and there heard the crying of the babies. He secured the box and carried it and the babies to his cave, and there they lived for several years untroubled.

One day a hunter, chasing deer with dogs, went by that way and saw the children. He returned to town and told what he had seen, and it came to the ears of the old women. They, being afraid that the king would learn of the children's being there, made 'maruya', which is a kind of sweetmeat, and mixed poison with it. Then they went out to where the children were and gave them the poisoned sweets, so that they all died. When night came the enchanter was greatly troubled because the children did not come, and taking a torch he set out to look for them. He found the little bodies lying at the foot of a tree, and wept long and bitterly. At last he took them to his cave and laid them in a row on the floor and wept again.

As he lamented he heard the voice of the oracle, which was like a beautiful woman's voice, accompanied by a harp, singing most sweetly, and bidding him beg a medicine of the mother of the Sun, who lives in the house of the Sun across seven mountains to the west. This, she promised, would restore them to life.

So he set out on his long journey, and when he had crossed three mountains he came to a tree on which the birds never lit, and the tree was lamenting the fact. The enchanter inquired the way to the Sun's house and the tree told him thus and so, but begged him to ask the mother of the Sun why the birds never lit on it. The enchanter went on, and on the next mountain he saw two men sitting in a pair of balances, which pitched up and down like a *banca* in a storm. From them he asked again the way to the Sun's house, and they told him and asked him to speak to the mother of the Sun as to why they were condemned to ride the limb of a tree like a boat in a storm.

He went on to the next mountain and there he saw two poor, lean cattle feeding on rich grass. From them also he inquired the direction of the Sun's house, and they told him and requested that he ask the mother of the Sun why they were always lean and fed on rich herbage. He promised and passed on to the next mountain, and there he saw a black ox eating nothing but earth and still fat and sleek. This animal told him how to find the Sun's house and wished to know of the mother of the Sun why he was always fat though he ate only dust.

The enchanter gave his word and went on. At last, late in the afternoon, he arrived at the Sun's house and went boldly upstairs. The mother of the Sun met him and inquired his business, which he told her, and then she told him that he was in great danger, for if her son, the Sun, came home and found him there he would eat him. The enchanter told her that he would not go away without the medicine, and at last the mother of the Sun agreed to hide him; so she wrapped him up so that the Sun could not smell him when he came in and carried him up to the seventh story of the house. There he was to remain until the next morning after the Sun had started off on his journey across the Heavens.

Soon the Sun came in and asked his mother where the man was, but his mother told him there was none and gave him such a fine supper that he forgot about the man, though he remarked once or twice that he certainly thought he smelled man. At last morning came, and when the Sun was far enough away to leave no danger, the mother of the Sun gave the enchanter the medicine that he wanted and started him off on his long journey. She told him, too, the answer to the questions asked by the cattle, the men, and the tree.

When he came to the black ox which lived on the dust, he told it that it was always fat because it was going to Heaven, and it was glad.

To the two oxen which fed on rich pasture and yet were poor, he said that they were so because they were condemned to Hell, and they were sorrowful.

To the men sitting in the pair of balances, he said that they were there because of their sins, and they became sad.

To the tree on which the birds never lit, he said that it was because it was made out of silver and gold, and the tree rustled its leaves in pride.

Finally he came to his cave, and there instead of the bodies of seven young children he saw the bodies of seven handsome young men, for they had grown greatly while he was away. He gave them the medicine, and they at once stood up. Then he told them all of his adventures.

When the boys heard the story, the youngest, who was a dare-devil, set out to find the gold and silver tree and from its branches he shook down a great quantity of gold and silver leaves, which he carried back to the enchanter. The enchanter was proud of the boy and yet angry with him for his rashness, but no one could be angry with him for long, for he was a gentle lad.

The enchanter then took the gold and silver and made clothes for them of cloth of gold, silver sabres, golden belts, and a golden trumpet for the youngest, and sent them away on a Sunday morning to church in the city where the king lived. As they came up close to the city wall, the trumpeter lad blew a merry blast on his horn, and the king sent out to inquire who they might be and to invite them to dinner after church. So they went to the palace after church and sat down to the king's table, and the dishes were brought on. The enchanter had warned them to eat nothing until they had fed a little to a dog, and one of the boys gave some meat to a dog that was with them. The dog was dead in a moment.

The king, ashamed, ordered everything to be changed and new cooks put into the kitchen, for of course he knew nothing of the wickedness against his sons, whom he did not recognize as yet. The boys now very respectfully requested that the woman chained in the hut be brought to the table with them, though they did not know why they should ask such a thing. So the king took his sword and with his own hands, from shame, set his wife free, and had her dressed as a queen and brought to the table. The jewel still glowed on her forehead. As they sat at the table, a stream of milk miraculously coming from the breast of the mother passed to the mouth of the youngest son. Then the king understood, and when he had heard the story of the sons he put the queen again into her rightful place and caused the wicked stepmother and her two accomplices to be pulled to pieces by wild horses.

The king, the queen, and the seven princes, having made an end of their rivals, lived long and happily together.

The Black Cat

Source: 'Le Chat Noir' in F. M. Luzel, *Contes Populaires de Basse-Bretagne*, vol. 3, Paris: Maisonneuve et Ch. Leclerc, 1887 (vol. 26 of *Les Littératures populaires de toutes les nations*). Told in Breton by Pierre Le Roux, baker in the village of Plouaret, December 1869. Translated from the French by Neil Philip with Nicoletta Simborowski.

This is in some ways a confused and confusing tale, a clumsy portmanteau story in which, for instance, the helpful animal takes four separate forms, in which there are three overlapping villains, and in which the role of the prince is split between two characters – one of whom, Rio, is far from heroic. However this doubling and tripling of roles is also a source of strength, allowing themes of treachery, jealousy, vengeance, and persecuted virtue to be amplified and intensified in various examples. The opening is standard, with the wicked stepmother, spoiled stepsister, weak father, and the black cow which the girl must tend. Then, however, the storyteller spirals off into related images, in which, for instance, the horrifying Lady Macbeth figure of Rio's murderous mistress offers another vantage point on the stepmother. This second half of the story, in which the girl gives birth to an animal helper who is really a powerful magician, is known as 'The Wonder-Child' (AT708): John Sampson collected a particularly powerful English gypsy version, 'De Little Fox'. Luzel notes that the duel between the cat and the witch resembles a Breton children's game, in which the children first blow, then spit in each other's faces, then chase each other with sticks from the fire.

In his recent selection from Luzel's Breton tales, *Celtic Folk-Tales from Armorica*, Derek Bryce translates a shorter version of this story, collected from Marguerite Philippe of Plouaret in 1869, under the title 'The Cat and the Two Witches'.

THERE WAS ONCE a widower, who married a widow. They each already had a child from their previous marriages, two girls of roughly the same age. The man's was called Yvonne, and was as sweet, kind and pretty as the other, who was called Louise, was ugly, wicked and insufferable. As usually happens in such cases, each parent liked their own child best, and kept their love and caresses for her.

The two young girls were by now sixteen or seventeen, and as their parents were well off, the young men of the district started visiting the house. The mother always showed off her daughter Louise, and was constantly buying her new dresses and costly finery, while Yvonne was meanly dressed. For all that, the suitors only had eyes and compliments for Yvonne, who was as modest and as good as she was pretty. Her stepmother was so full of jealousy and resentment that she decided to send the girl away and remove her from the sight of the suitors, so that her own daughter could marry first. Each day she sent her to a wide moor to look after a little black cow, with orders not to come back before sunset. The poor child left each morning at dawn, without complaint, with just a bit of black bread and a biscuit to eat. Because she was always with the cow, and had no other company, save a little dog called Fidèle, who followed her everywhere, she was fond of the cow, and thought of it as her best friend. She fed it fresh herbs from her hand, which she selected and gathered herself; she petted it, stroked its head, kissed it, told it a thousand little stories, and sang it such songs as she knew: and the beast looked at her through steady gentle eyes, and seemed to understand, and to love her back. She called it: *My little golden heart.*

The cow, which had been lean and puny when first put in Yvonne's charge, grew plump and sleek, thanks to the young girl's care. The stepmother noticed this one day, and also Yvonne's love for the cow, and straight away said the beast must be killed, as she wanted to give a feast.

The cow was killed, and Yvonne suffered a great sadness. When the cow was cut open, there was found next to the heart a pair of little golden slippers, made with marvellous skill. The stepmother took them, saying: 'These will be for my daughter, the day she weds.'

Some days later, a very rich prince, who had heard tell of the beauty and sweet nature of Yvonne, came to see her. The stepmother, with an evil purpose, made her put on Louise's clothes, jewels and diamonds, and then presented her to the prince. He talked with her a while, and he was so charmed with her beauty and her conversation that he said he wanted no other wife but her. And he asked for her hand. There was no question of refusing him, and the marriage-day was set then and there. Then the prince returned to his kingdom.

No doubt you can guess the betrayal that wicked woman had in mind: to substitute her daughter for that of her husband. On the morning of the appointed day, Yvonne was locked up in a turret-room, while Louise, who was to take her place, was clothed in the most expensive raiment, without nevertheless turning her into a beautiful bride-to-be. When they tried to fit her with the golden slippers found in the body of the black cow, they had to shorten her feet at both ends to get them in, by chopping off her heels and her toes.

The young prince arrived with a numerous and brilliant retinue. He was presented with the fake bride, and the light which sparkled from the gold and the diamonds with which she was covered blinded him, and stopped him recognizing the fraud. He hurriedly climbed with her into a fine gilded carriage, which he had brought for that purpose, and straight away the cortège left for the church. The little dog Fidèle, who used to go with Yvonne to the moor, when she took her black cow to graze there, was on the steps, and when he saw the prince climb into the carriage, with his supposed fiancée, he started to yap: *Hep-hi! hep-hi! hep-hi!* – that's to say 'Without her! without her! without her!' And when the carriage drove out of the courtyard, he ran after, saying in his language:

> *It is sullen ugly-nose*
> *With clipped heels and shorn toes*
> *Alas! alas! the pretty one*
> *Is left locked up to weep and moan!*

But no one paid the poor animal any attention.

When they got to the church door, the false bride had to step down from the carriage: but, alas! she could not walk any more, and at each step she attempted, she gave cries of pain. The prince, seeing her in broad daylight, could not keep back his cry of astonished indignation, and, recoiling as at the sight of a monster, he cried: 'Treachery! This is not she whom I saw, whom I love: go home; take this monster from my sight!'

You can imagine his shock and distress.

The prince was furious, and left straight away with all his retinue. Louise's mother went home with her daughter, who wept hot tears to be returning in that fashion, after having been so nearly married to a prince. She foamed with rage, the wicked woman, and swore a terrible vengeance.

Even before reaching home she sought out an old witch who lived in a wood nearby. She told the witch of her misfortune, and the old devil soothed her and promised to put all her knowledge at her service, and to be her friend.

'Go back to the house,' the witch told her, 'kill a black cat which is in your château, cook it like jugged hare, and give it to the beautiful Yvonne to eat; you'll not have to worry about her again. She will find it delicious, she'll go to sleep without a care, and next day you'll find her dead in her bed.'

'Good,' said the wicked woman.

And she kissed her friend the witch, and went back home.

When she got back, she herself caught the black cat, killed it, skinned it, and prepared it as jugged hare. Then, when she thought it done to a turn, she put the stew on a plate and carried it herself to Yvonne in her room.

'How are you, my daughter?' she asked her, with a hypocritical air, pretending the best of feelings for her. 'We have hare for dinner today, and, as I know you're partial to it, I wanted you to have your share. Take it, my dear daughter, and eat it. I prepared it myself, and it must be good, for I used all my skill.'

Poor Yvonne, who never thought ill of anyone, believed that her stepmother perhaps regretted having treated her so harshly, and not doubting the sincerity of the good wishes which she showed to her, she was completely happy. She ate the stew without hesitation, and thought it excellent. The stepmother left her, satisfied, revelling already in her vengeance. Almost immediately, the young girl felt ill, and had to lie down, before her usual bedtime. All night, she was deathly ill. She threw up everything she had eaten, and it was that, no doubt, that saved her.

The next morning early, the stepmother ran to her room, and was astonished to find her still alive. But hiding her disappointment, and hatred, she asked her in a loving tone: 'Did you sleep well, dear? You are pale, and I'm afraid you must have been bilious, from eating too much stew yesterday.'

'Oh! mother,' answered Yvonne, 'I've been very ill, very ill; I almost died, last night.'

'Poor child! But happily it's not anything; you're getting your colour back already.'

And the wicked, accursed serpent, unable to hide her fury any longer, left and ran to her friend the witch. She told her that her cat stew had failed, because the young girl still lived. The other snake was stunned to learn that, for this method had never failed her before.

'What's to do now? I must find another way, and quick,' said the stepmother.

'Well! I see no other way than to make life impossible for your husband and his daughter. Be in a bad mood all the time; nag; threaten; even beat; feed them badly, on what they like least. Make your house hell for them, and they will eventually leave it and go of their own accord to some distant land.'

The stepmother went home with her friend's advice and started straight away to put it into practice. Truly neither her husband nor his daughter had ever had cause to praise either her character or her behaviour in their regard; but from that moment, she was a real fury, and they were obliged to think of ways of getting away from her. The father and daughter planned to cross the sea, and go as far away as they could. They got hold of a small boat, and one night they left in secret and went to the nearest shore. But, just as they were about to set sail, they saw the wicked woman running towards them, making signs with her hands and crying to her husband: 'Stop! stop! where are you going in this mad way? Don't you realize, scatterbrain, that you've forgotten to take your little red book? You know well enough that you can't do anything without it; come back and fetch it from the house, you poor imbecile, and then I'll let you go where you like with your daughter.'

The poor man, used for so long to blind obedience to his wife, and to never contradicting her, didn't dare continue on his way, and didn't see the trap that was set for him. He stepped back on to the shore, moored his boat to a post, and went back to the château to fetch his little red book. His wife promised to wait by the boat, in which Yvonne was left alone. But hardly was she out of his sight than the stepmother untied the rope, and the boat moved away smartly on a brisk land breeze, carrying off the poor girl, despite her cries and wails. We'll follow her, and leave the wicked stepmother and her daughter; we'll go back to them later.

After journeying many days and nights at the mercy of the tides and the winds, the boat came to shore at last on a small island. Yvonne, who had given herself up for lost, regained hope, and started to explore the island in search of a house. But she found neither house nor householder; the island was deserted. As she walked sadly by the shore, she noticed among the rocks something that looked like the door of a human habitation. She approached it, struck it with a stick she held in her hand, and the door opened easily. There she saw a cave, which looked inhabited, having various necessaries, such as a stewpot and a water jug, a bowl and some wooden plates, and lastly a modest bed; but there was no other living creature anywhere.

'It must be a hermitage,' she told herself.

She sat down on a stool to wait for the hermit, who she assumed to have retired to this solitude as a penance. But after waiting a long while, as no one had come and she was hungry, she went to walk by the shore. There she found many shellfish of every sort, which she ate quite raw. At sunset, she went back to the cave, but still found no one there. As she was tired, she decided therefore to go to sleep on the bed with all her clothes on. She slept soundly all night, and when she awoke next morning, she was still alone.

'The hermitage must have been abandoned,' she told herself. 'My best course is to move in.'

All day she explored the island, making sure it was completely deserted. She gathered shellfish by the shore and cooked them for her supper. Then she went to bed, less troubled than the previous day, and slept till the next morning, without anything else disturbing her rest.

The island also provided various fruits, so that she found each day's food easily enough: and she had neither glimpsed nor heard any wild beast to make her afraid. She was truly mistress and queen of the island, and apart from the complete solitude in which she found herself, she had no reason to miss her stepmother's house.

One day after three weeks of this existence, she felt unwell. She thought it was the shellfish or the fruit she had eaten. Imagine her amazement when she discovered she was pregnant! She couldn't explain it. She took to her bed in great distress, and in the morning gave birth to a black kitten. At first she couldn't believe her eyes; but when it was clear that it was truly a cat and not a child, she said resignedly: 'God has sent him to me; I must accept him without complaint, as God's gift, and treat him as my child, because that is His wish.'

She offered her breast to the kitten, and he sucked, just like a child. She soon became used to thinking of him as her son, and she loved him as if he was. She played with him, and walked with him on the island, and he was comfort and company for her in her loneliness. The cat grew fast, and showed great intelligence. After two or three months it was a splendid black cat, such as you rarely see. One day, to his mother's great surprise, he spoke up, just like a man: 'I know, my poor mother, all that you have suffered for me so far, and the unhappiness you still feel to see me made in this way: but cheer up, for though your son is a black cat, or looks like one, you won't always be ashamed of me. One day your goodness and love will be recognized, and you will be revenged on those who have done you such harm and would still like to do more. While waiting, Mother, make me a knapsack I can wear on my shoulders, and I will go and forage for you in the nearest town, and bring you something better than the mussels, limpets, clams and other shell-fish which have been your sole food since you have been on this island.'

'Jesus! my poor child,' cried Yvonne, more astonished than ever, 'how is it that you talk like this, just like a man, even though you look like a cat?'

'I can't say now, Mother, but one day you will know.'

'I know, child, that God does as He wills, and that we must find His actions good. But I'm afraid to let you go alone from our island; you might come to harm. And how will you cross the sea?'

'Don't fear, Mother, nothing bad will happen to me, because I am risking myself for love of you; and as for crossing the sea, that's not hard for me, because I can swim like a fish.'

Yvonne let herself be persuaded by the cat's arguments, and she made him a knapsack as he asked. The cat slung it on his shoulders, plunged into the sea, and, as he had said, he swam like a fish, which reassured his mother, who followed him with her eyes from the shore.

He made land without mishap, and arrived at a sea-port such as Lannion or Treguier. As he made his way towards the town, along the quayside, schoolboys saw him. 'Look! look! look at that funny cat, with a knap-sack on his back, like a beggar,' they said to each other, pointing their fingers at him.

And they ran after the cat, throwing stones at him. The animal dived through the first open door. It was the house of Mr Rio, one of the richest men in town. He stopped at the kitchen door and started to cry: *Miaou! miaou!* The cook, seeing a big black cat whom she didn't recognize as belonging to any of the neighbours, took her broom to chase him away; but she was amazed to hear him coolly ask: 'Is Mr Rio at home?'

She let her broom fall to the ground in surprise, and then, when the cat repeated his question, answered, 'No, he's not at home at present, but he'll be back soon, for dinner.'

'I haven't time to wait,' replied the cat, 'so I'll thank you to hurry and put that chicken I see on the spit into my knapsack, along with a good slice of bacon.'

'What? What? Give you this chicken, which is my master's dinner? There's no hope of that, Mr Cat.'

'I must have it; and also, I want some white bread and a bottle of old wine. Be so kind as to put all that in my knapsack.'

As the cook hesitated, the cat took the chicken from the spit himself, then took a good slice of bacon which was on a plate on the kitchen table, and a bottle of old wine that was by it, put the lot in his knapsack, slung it on his shoulders and left, saying to the girl, who was dumbstruck by what she had seen and heard, goodbye, he was sure to be back. He slipped along garden walls and behind hedges, and arrived without accident at the shore, where he plunged into the sea and made haste back to the island and his mother. She was waiting for him by the shore, not without anxiety. So when she spied him swimming towards her, she let out a cry of joy. 'I'm so happy to have you back, my son!' she told him, kissing him tenderly as he came on land.

'Look, Mother,' said the cat, opening his knapsack, 'I've brought provisions, as I promised: something a bit better, I think, than the limpets, mussels and other shellfish which have for so long been our only food. Let's set to, and when that's finished, I know where to get more.'

And they set to, while the provisions lasted.

Meanwhile, when Mr Rio got home and saw there was nothing on the table or on the stove, he asked sharply of the cook, who was still flabbergasted: 'Why isn't dinner ready? And I was afraid of being late! What have you been up to?'

'Oh! master,' answered the poor girl, 'if you knew what's been going on here.'

'Well, what? What's happened that's so special?'

'A big black cat came here, with a knapsack on his shoulders, and said to me – it was a wizard or magician to be sure – that he needed the chicken that was on the spit, for your dinner, and a good slice of bacon, some white bread and a bottle of old wine; and as I'd picked up my broom to chase him, went over to the chicken and took it off the spit himself, and put it in his knapsack; then, he took a slice of bacon too, and a bottle of old wine, and left, carrying the lot, and promising me he'd return, without delay.'

'Come, come. What fairytale are you telling me? Do you take me for an imbecile?'

Mr Rio was furious. But the cook swore with such conviction that everything she said was strictly true, and cried so much, that he calmed down, and, as the cat had promised to return before long, he stayed in the house, to see for himself what to make of such a strange happening.

Soon the provisions on the island were all gone, and the cat put his knapsack back on his shoulders and set off once again to the town where Mr Rio lived. His mother watched him go with less anxiety this time. He arrived in the town without mishap, and went straight to Mr Rio's house. He stopped at the kitchen door, as before, and went: *Miaou! miaou!*

'Master! master!' shouted the cook, who recognized him straight away. 'Come quick: here's the black cat come back!'

Rio came down from his room, with his loaded gun in his hand. The cat wasn't at all scared to see him, but just stared at him and continued to mew: *Miaou! miaou!*

'Ah! It's you, you mangy tom!' shouted Rio. 'You're going to have this out with me, here and now!'

'I'm not afraid of you,' said the cat coolly. 'Watch out for yourself.'

Wasn't Rio flummoxed to hear a cat talk to him like a man, and threaten him.

'What do you want?' he asked, calming down and speaking more gently.

'Like the first time, I want some meat, white bread and wine, for my mother and myself.'

'Oh! You need meat, bread and old wine, Sir cat,' responded Rio, ashamed to be afraid of a cat, especially with a loaded gun in his hand. 'Well! Don't worry. Instead of meat, bread and wine, I'm going to give you a bullet in the body, and we'll see the faces you'll pull.'

And he took aim. But the cat flew at his face and set his claws and his teeth in the flesh.

'Mercy! mercy! let me go, and I'll give you what you want,' cried Rio.

'That's what I like to hear,' said the cat, leaping to the ground. 'And to prove I don't bear ill will, I'll even give you some useful advice. I know all about you, Mr Rio. I know you have a mistress, whom you see often and who you think loves you, because she tells you so. But the woman doesn't love you, and she's planning, at this moment, a vile betrayal, with the help of another lover she likes better than you. Listen well, and if you do exactly as I tell you, you can escape the trap she is preparing for you. One day soon, the woman you visit will give a hunting party, followed by a banquet. You will be invited, that goes without saying; but your rival will be there too. You'll catch more game than any other hunter, and everybody will congratulate you; but the woman and her lover will be full of spite and jealousy. As there won't be a bed for every hunter, they'll sleep in pairs. Your bed-companion will be your rival himself. Watch out, I tell you again, or you'll lose your life that very night. After the meal, at which everyone will be drinking, when it is time for bed you'll go to your room with your enemy. He'll be drunk and sleepy. He'll be in bed first, next to the wall, and instantly asleep. Go to bed yourself, without seeming troubled by anything, but be careful not to doze off. When your companion starts to snore, change places with him, pushing him across so you are on the wall side, then put out the light and pretend to snore yourself. When the woman thinks you are both deep asleep, she'll go into your room, so quietly, on tiptoe, with a big knife, which she will have whetted to an edge that day, and she'll cut the neck of the sleeper on the outside of the bed, thinking it is you. Then she'll go, giving a kick at the severed head which will roll on the floor. Have you got that? Good! be on your guard, and do exactly as I say, or it'll be the worse for you! . . . Something else may happen to you afterwards, but trust me, and I'll come to your help, at the right time.'

Rio was astonished and frightened at what he heard. He thanked the cat very much, and refilled his knapsack with the best he could find, telling him to come back when his provisions were exhausted. Then the cat went back to his mother's side, on the island.

As for Rio, he thought a lot about what he'd heard, and even considered refusing the invitation to the hunting party at his mistress's château. But he went all the same, saying that he'd be a right fool to be intimidated by a cat, and that no doubt he'd been hallucinating, and dreamed the whole thing, as it seemed strange and supernatural that a cat should speak and reason in that way.

All the honours of the day were his, and he slew a prodigious quantity of game of all sorts. The meal that evening was magnificent, and the mistress of the château never stopped saying gracious and admiring things to him. They drank such healths that, when the hour for bed arrived, their heads were a bit fuddled, and they were talking long and loud. Rio went up to his room, with the companion that the hostess herself had picked out, who had been drinking heavily. The man went straight to bed, and some minutes later started to snore like an organ pipe. Rio went to bed too, on the outside of the bed, and very nearly fell asleep straight away. Luckily, he remembered the cat's advice in time. He changed places with his companion in the bed, without waking him, for he was sleeping like a log, put him on the outside, and took the place by the wall. Then he put out the light, and pretended to sleep and snore too.

Soon after, he heard the door of the room slowly open, and saw the hostess, his mistress, tiptoe in and approach the bed. She held in one hand a candle, and in the other, a great hunting knife. When she reached the bed, without a moment's hesitation, she sliced the head from the sleeper on the outside, thinking it was Rio, and let it roll on the floor, and kicked it with her foot. She left, and double-locked the door.

Rio was in a tight place as you'll realize. He thought of escaping by a window, by the door, or by any other exit he could find. But the windows had thick iron bars, which he couldn't squeeze between, and the door was locked. He had to spend the night with a headless corpse bathed in its blood. He was very worried about what would happen next day, and said to himself: 'If the black cat doesn't come to my aid again, I'm lost, and it won't do me any good to have saved my head tonight, as surely this she-devil won't miss the chance of accusing me of this man's murder!'

Next morning, the sun had been up a long time, and everybody in the château was up and about, but Rio and his companion hadn't come down. Sitting down for breakfast, the hostess, pretending not to know the reason, asked news of them, and was told that nobody had seen them since the day before.

'Lazybones!' she said. 'Let's go and find them in their room and find out what sort of a night they had – perhaps they're not feeling well.'

And she went up to their room, followed by half-a-dozen of the hunters. When she opened the door and saw her error, saw Rio standing up, waiting for someone to open up, and the head of the other drowned in blood, and his body sprawling by its side, she let out a wild cry and almost fainted. But, overcoming her grief, and not losing sight of her revenge she cried: 'Oh! the scoundrel. He has killed his night's companion. Tie him up and throw him in jail; tomorrow he'll die on the scaffold.'

The servants were called, and poor Rio was bound and roughly thrown into the bottom of a dungeon, to be taken from there to his death, next morning.

A scaffold was set up in the middle of the château courtyard, and the next morning, at ten o'clock, Rio was fetched from his prison and made to climb it. The woman was on her balcony, surrounded by her companions of the day before, and all the windows were full of spectators. Looking from side to side in despair, Rio noticed the black cat on a roof, and straight away a glimmer of hope lit up his face. Turning to the animal, he said: 'Since I've no more hope in men, if that black cat which I see up there would only help me and reveal the truth, I wouldn't die today!'

Immediately all eyes turned on the cat. It sprang on to the scaffold next to Rio, and spoke to the headsman, who, axe on shoulder, only awaited the signal to strike: 'Whoa! hold it, friend! This man is innocent. It's not him you should strike, but the real guilty party, who committed this crime: her over there!'

And he pointed at the mistress of the château, on her balcony, dressed for a holiday and surrounded by admirers. She paled, let out a cry, and fainted. Imagine the amazement of everyone there!

So Rio got down from the scaffold, and the woman was made to climb it, to be beheaded in his place, despite her pleas and moans; for no one dared defend her or speak in her favour, they were all so terrified of the black cat. When it was all over, Rio went home, happy to have escaped. The black cat, too, returned to his island.

Some days later, the cat told his mother, 'Mother, you must get married.'

'What? Me, marry? Who would want me, Son?'

'I've found you a husband, Mother. You will be the bride of Mr Rio, whose life I saved. Trust me, and I will arrange it all.'

The next day, the cat went back to Mr Rio's house, and told him straight, 'Hello, Mr Rio. You must marry my mother.'

'Marry your mother, friend! A cat!'

'Yes, you've got to marry her.'

'I know I owe you my life; for all that, whatever debt I owe you, if the price is to marry a cat . . .'

'Believe me, Mr Rio, my mother is worthy of you; marry her, and you won't regret it, I tell you.'

'Perhaps when I've seen her . . . Then we'll see . . .'

'I'll bring her to you tomorrow.'

And with that the cat departed, leaving Rio in a terrible fix. He was afraid to upset the cat, and seem ungrateful; but on the other hand, he couldn't come to terms with the notion of marrying a cat.

The cat, after leaving the house, slipped down the guttering into a rich marquise's bedroom, and stole dresses of silk and velvet, every sort of jewel and diamonds, and, putting the lot in his knapsack, returned to the island. This time he was taken by a ferryman, in order to fetch his mother, next day.

Despite her misfortunes, Yvonne had lost none of her beauty. She put on the beautiful clothes and costly jewels which the cat had brought her, and no human eye has ever seen a princess more beautiful, gracious and elegant. The cat took her to Mr Rio's house, as he'd promised, and introduced her, saying: 'Mr Rio, meet my mother: do you agree to marry her?'

Mr Rio was dazzled by Yvonne's beauty, her grace, her clothes. At first he couldn't reply, his voice failed him. But he soon recovered, and said, 'Yes, with all my heart, I agree to take your mother for my wife, and think myself the happiest of men.'

The betrothal was made that day, and the wedding was fixed for eight days later, leaving time to prepare everything and send out invitations. On the day there were games and feasting on a grand scale, and all of the people from the town and the surrounding district were there, rich and poor! The black cat followed the new bride everywhere, and as no one except Rio and Yvonne knew the secret, everyone thought that very remarkable.

When the ceremony, the games and the feasting were over, the cat told his mother, 'I don't yet know my grandfather, or my grandmother, or your sister Louise, and I'm dying to meet them; the three of us must go and pay them a wedding visit.'

So next morning the three of them got in a fine carriage and set off.

Yvonne's father, her stepmother and Louise were still alive, and living together. Her father received them with sincere joy and happiness; the stepmother and her daughter, who was still unmarried, pretended to be delighted to see them too – but really they were full of spite and jealousy. However, they prepared a grand feast to celebrate, and invited many people. The old witch of the wood wasn't forgotten. But during the meal, recognizing the black cat who loitered round the table, the witch turned pale, pretended to be ill, and left. Then the black cat jumped on the table, tail bushy and eyes flaring.

'Get out, you vile beast!' shouted the stepmother.

'Ha!' replied the cat. 'I'd like to see you make me!'

The old woman kept quiet. All the revellers were astonished and frightened, except Mr Rio and his wife.

'There's someone missing,' said the cat.

'Who?' asked the stepmother.

'Your friend the witch, who pretended to be ill and left. Someone run after her and bring her back, now.'

Servants ran after the witch, and soon caught her and brought her back into the dining hall, despite her struggles, her pleas and her threats.

'Silence, you old snake, you hell-brand!' shouted the cat, and she shook all over.

The cat continued, 'Judgement day has come for you. You must fight me, and you know what you'll get if you lose.'

'I'll fight, as you like,' replied the witch with a show of confidence, 'and I don't fear you by water, wind or fire!'

'We'll see about that.'

'As you like.'

'Well! Let's go into the courtyard. Everyone here will witness the fight from the balconies and windows of the château, and judge who is the victor.'

And the black cat and the old witch went into the courtyard, and all the people went to the windows.

'How shall we start,' asked the witch, when they were in the courtyard, facing each other.

'How you like,' said the cat.

'Well, let's start with water.'

They began to vomit water at each other, each doing their best. But for every barrelful the witch spewed out, the cat vomited three. She was soon forced to beg for mercy and admit defeat in that contest.

'Let's try wind now,' she said.

They began to blow furiously at each other. But the wind produced by the witch was nothing to that of the cat, who blew the old woman about like a straw, to the right, to the left, against the walls, till she hurried to shout again, 'Mercy! mercy!'

So she was defeated twice.

'And now it's the turn of fire!' said the black cat.

And they began to vomit fire at each other, like two enraged dragons, or two devils from hell. But for every flame spewed out by the witch, the black cat vomited three, so that she was burnt to ashes.

'Good!' said the cat. 'You have got what you deserved.'

And he went back into the dining hall. The spectators left the balconies and windows and followed him.

'One has paid the price,' he said, 'but there's still another I don't want to forget.'

And he spoke to the stepmother, who was white and trembling in every limb, as she felt her hour had also come: 'We must pay you out too; it's your turn, Madam.'

'What for, please, Sir cat?'

'For all your kindness to my mother.'

'To your mother?'

'Yes, my mother here' – he motioned to Yvonne – 'don't you remember now your jugged hare?'

The wicked woman wished herself a hundred feet under the ground at that moment. The cat vomited fire all over her too, as in his fight with the witch, and in an instant reduced her to cinders too.

Then he approached Louise, who, thinking her hour had come, was in a deathly trance.

'As for you, my girl, I won't do you any harm. You were too young to understand what you were about. It was your mother alone who was guilty.'

Lastly he said to Mr Rio: 'Now, Mr Rio, put me on my back on the table and slit me open with your sword.'

'I can't do that,' replied Mr Rio.

'Do as I tell you, and don't be afraid.'

And Mr Rio took the black cat, stretched him on his back on the table and with his sword he slit his stomach.

Out stepped a handsome prince, who said, 'I am the greatest magician who ever lived on earth!'

They went back to drinking, singing and dancing, and the feasting, fun and merrymaking lasted eight whole days.

The Maiden, the Frog and the Chief's Son

Source: William Bascom 'Cinderella in Africa', *Journal of the Folklore Institute*, 9, 1972, collected by Frank Edgar. Translated from the Hausa by Neil Skinner, Bloomington, Indiana, Indiana University Folklore Institute.

This tale was recorded by a British colonial administrator, Francis Edgar, who served in Northern Nigeria from 1905 to 1927. Edgar collected many Hausa narratives, publishing them in the original Hausa in the three volumes of *Litafi na Tatsuniyoyi na Hausa* (1911–13), since when his published and unpublished material has been variously drawn on, culminating in Neil Skinner's magnificent translation, *Hausa Tales and Traditions*.

'The Maiden, the Frog and the Chief's Son' is discussed in an important critical article by William Bascom, 'Cinderella in Africa', which is reprinted in full in Dundes's *Cinderella: A Folklore Casebook*. Bascom concludes that the Cinderella tale has entered Hausa tradition via European influence. This seems to be the case with all Cinderellas or quasi-Cinderellas reported from Africa, though, as in this case, they quickly adopt a cultural camouflage which makes them seem absolutely natural. This is particularly obvious in the story of 'Sindela' collected in 1969 by Clement A. Okafor among the Tonga of Southern Nigeria, which is abstracted as Narrative no. 1 in his study *The Banished Child*. The European origin of the tale is clear; Okafor's informant, an agricultural officer, learnt the story from a foreign anthology. This is how it runs:

Sindela is born into a polygamous family. When Sindela's mother dies, the mother's co-wife begins to maltreat Sindela and forces her to minister to her own children. One day, Sindela's dead mother, assuming the guise of a soul-bird, appears to Sindela, and equips her with beautiful clothes which enable her to attract the attention of a prince. He eventually marries her and saves her from the misery in her home.

In 'The Maiden, the Frog and the Chief's Son', *fura* and *tuwo* are respectively the morning and evening meals. The closing sentence, *Kungurus kan kusu*, is a traditional story ending. It probably means 'The rat's head is off.'

THERE WAS ONCE a man had two wives, and they each had a daughter. And the one wife, together with her daughter, he couldn't abide; but the other, with her daughter, he dearly loved.

Well, the day came when the wife that he disliked fell ill, and it so happened that her illness proved fatal, and she died. And her daughter was taken over by the other wife, the one he loved; and she moved into that wife's hut. And there she dwelt, having no mother of her own, just her father. And every day the woman would push her out, to go off to the bush to gather wood. When she returned, she had to fetch water. And when she finished that she had to pound up the *fura*. Then she had the *tuwo* to pound, and, after that, to stir. And then they wouldn't even let her eat the *tuwo*. All they gave her to eat were the burnt bits at the bottom of the pot. And day after day she continued thus.

Now she had an elder brother, and he invited her to come and eat regularly at his home – to which she agreed. But still when she had been to the bush, and returned home, and wanted a drink of water, they wouldn't let her have one. Nor would they give her proper food – only the coarsest of the grindings and the scrapings from the pot. These she would take, and going with them to a borrow-pit, throw them in. And the frogs would come out and start eating the scrapings. Then, having eaten them up, they would go back into the water; and she too would return home.

And so things went on day after day, until the day of the Festival arrived. And on this day, when she went along with the scrapings and coarse grindings, she found a frog squatting there; and realized that he was waiting for her! She got there and threw in the bits of food.

Whereupon the frog said, 'Maiden, you've always been very kind to us, and now we – but just you come along tomorrow morning. That's the morning of the Festival. Come along then, and we'll be kind to you, in our turn.' 'Fine,' she said, and went off home.

Next morning was the Festival, and she was going off to the borrow-pit, just as the frog had told her. But as she was going, her half-sister's mother said to her, 'Hey – come here, you good-for-nothing girl! You

haven't stirred the *tuwo*, or pounded the *fura*, or fetched the wood or the water.' So the girl returned. And the frog spent the whole day waiting for her. But she, having returned to the compound, set off to fetch wood. Then she fetched water, and set about pounding the *tuwo*, and stirred it till it was done and then took it off the fire. And presently she was told to take the scrapings. She did so and went off to the borrow-pit, where she found the frog. 'Tut tut, girl,' said he, 'I've been waiting for you here since morning, and you never came.' 'Old fellow,' she said, 'you see, I'm a slave.' 'How come?' he asked. 'Simple,' she said, 'my mother died – died leaving me her only daughter. I have an elder brother, but he is married and has a compound of his own. And my father put me in the care of his other wife. And indeed he had never loved my mother. So I was moved into the hut of his other wife. And, as I told you, slavery is my lot. Every morning I have to go off to the bush to get wood. When I get back from that I have to pound the *fura*, and then I pound the *tuwo*, and then start stirring it. And even when I have finished stirring the *tuwo*, I'm not given it to eat – just the scrapings.' Says the frog, 'Girl, give us your

139

hand.' And she held it out to him, and they both leaped into the water.

Then he went and picked her up and swallowed her. (And he vomited her up.) 'Good people,' said he, 'look and tell me, is she straight or crooked?' And they looked and answered, 'She is bent to the left.' So he picked her up and swallowed her again and then brought her up, and again asked them the same question. 'She's quite straight now,' they said. 'Good,' said he.

Next he vomited up cloths for her, and bangles, and rings, and a pair of shoes, one of silver, one of gold. 'And now,' said he, 'off you go to the dancing.' So all these things were given to her, and he said to her, 'When you get there, and when the dancing is nearly over and the dancers dispersing, you're to leave your golden shoe, the right one, there.' And the girl replied to the frog, 'Very well, old fellow, I understand,' and off she went.

Meanwhile the chief's son had caused the young men and girls to dance for his pleasure, and when she reached the space where they were dancing he saw her. 'Well!' said the chief's son, '*there's* a maiden for you, if you like. Don't you let her go and join in the dancing – I don't care whose home she comes from. Bring her here!' So the servants of the chief's son went over and came back with her to where he was. He told her to sit down on the couch, and she took her seat there accordingly.

They chatted together for some time, till the dancers began to disperse. Then she said to the chief's son, 'I must be going home.' 'Oh, are you off?' said he. 'Yes,' said she and rose to her feet. 'I'll accompany you on your way for a little,' said the chief's son, and he did so. But she had left her right shoe behind. Presently she said, 'Chief's son, you must go back now,' and he did so. And afterwards she too turned and made her way back.

And there she found the frog by the edge of the water waiting for her. He took her hand and the two of them jumped into the water. Then he picked her up and swallowed her, and again vomited her up; and there she was, just as she had been before, a sorry sight. And taking her ragged things she went off home.

When she got there, she said, 'Fellow-wife of my mother, I'm not feeling very well.' And the other said, 'Rascally slut! You have been up to no good – refusing to come home, refusing to fetch water or wood, refusing to pound the *fura* or make the *tuwo*. Very well then! No food for you today!' And so the girl set off to her elder brother's compound, and there ate her food, and so returned home again.

But meanwhile the chief's son had picked up the shoe and said to his father, 'Dad, I have seen a girl who wears a pair of shoes, one of gold, one of silver. Look, here's the golden one – she forgot it and left it behind. She's the girl I want to marry. So let all the girls of this town, young and old, be gathered together, and let this shoe be given to them to put on.' 'Very well,' said the chief.

And so it was proclaimed, and all the girls, young and old, were collected and gathered together. And the chief's son went and sat there beside the shoe. Each girl came, and each tried on the shoe, but it fitted none of the girls of the town; until only the girl who had left it was left. Then someone said, 'Just a minute! There's that girl in so-and-so's compound, whose mother died.' 'Yes, that's right,' said another, 'someone go and fetch her.' And someone went and fetched her.

But the minute she arrived to try it on, the shoe itself of its own accord ran across and made her foot get into it. Then said the chief's son, 'Right, here's my wife.'

At this, the other woman – the girl's father's other wife – said, 'But the shoe belongs to my daughter; it was she who forgot it at the place of the dancing, not this good-for-nothing slut.' But the chief's son insisted that, since he had seen the shoe fit the other girl, as far as he was concerned, she was the one to be taken to his compound in marriage. And so they took her there, and there she spent one night.

Next morning she went out of her hut and round behind it, and there saw the frog. She knelt respectfully and said, 'Welcome, old fellow, welcome,' and greeted him. Says he, 'Tonight we shall be along to bring some things for you.' 'Thank you,' said she, and he departed.

Well, that night, the frog rallied all the other frogs, and all his friends, both great and small came along. And he, their leader, said to them, 'See here – my daughter is being married. So I want every one of you to make a contribution.' And each of them went and fetched what he could afford, whereupon their leader thanked them all, and then vomited up a silver bed, a brass bed, a copper bed, and an iron bed. And went on vomiting up things for her – such as woollen blankets, and rugs, and satins, and velvets.

'Now,' said he to the girl, 'if your heart is ever troubled, just lie down on this brass bed,' and he went on, 'And when the chief's son's other wives come to greet you, give them two calabashes of cola-nuts and ten thousand cowrie shells; then, when his concubines come to greet you, give them one calabash of cola-nuts and five thousand cowries.' 'Very well,' said she. Then he said, 'And when the concubines come to receive corn for making *tuwo*, say to them, "There's a hide-bag full, help yourselves."' 'Very well,' she said. 'And,' he went on, 'if your father's wife comes along with her daughter and asks you what it is like living in the chief's compound, say "Living in the chief's compound is a wearisome business – for they measure out corn there with the shell of a Bambara groundnut."'

So there she dwelt, until one day her father's favourite wife brought her daughter along at night, took her into the chief's compound, and brought the other girl out and took her to her own compound. There she said, 'Oh! I forgot to get you to tell her all about married life in the chief's compound.' 'Oh, it's a wearisome business,' answered our girl. 'How so?' asked the older woman, surprised. 'Well, they use the shell of a Bambara groundnut for measuring out corn. Then, if the chief's other wives come to greet you, you answer them with the "Pf" of contempt. If the concubines come to greet you, you clear your throat, hawk, and spit. And if your husband comes into your hut, you yell at him.' 'I see,' said the other – and her daughter stayed behind in the chief's son's compound.

Next morning when it was light, the wives came to greet her – and she said 'Pf' to them. The concubines came to greet her, and she spat at them. Then when night fell, the chief's son made his way to her hut, and she yelled at him. And he was amazed and went aside, and for two days pondered the matter.

Then he had his wives and concubines collected and said to them, 'Look, now – I've called you to ask you. They haven't brought me the same girl. How did that one treat all of you?' 'Hm – how indeed!' they all exclaimed. 'Each morning, when we wives went to greet her, she would give us cola-nuts, two calabashes full, and cowries, ten thousand of them to buy tobacco flowers. And when the concubines went to greet her, she would give them a calabash of cola-nuts, and five thousand cowries to buy tobacco flowers with; and in the evening, for corn for *tuwo* it would be a whole hide-bag full.' 'You see?' said he. 'As for me, whenever I came to enter her hut, I found her respectfully kneeling. And she wouldn't get up from there, until I had entered and sat down on the bed.'

'Hey,' he called out. 'Boys, come over here!' And when they came, he went into her hut and took a sword, and chopped her up into little pieces, and had them collect them and wrap them up in clothing; and then taken back to her home.

And when they got there, they found his true wife lying in the fireplace, and picking her up they took her back to her husband.

And next morning when it was light, she picked up a little gourd water-bottle and going around behind her hut, there saw the frog. 'Welcome, welcome, old fellow,' said she, and went on, 'old fellow, what I should like is to have a well built; and then you, all of you, can come and live in it and be close to me.' 'All right,' said the frog. 'You tell your husband.' And she did so.

And he had a well dug for her, close to her hut. And the frogs came and entered the well and there they lived. That's all. *Kungurus kan kusu.*

Rushycoat and the King's Son

Source: Leonard Roberts, *Old Greasybeard: Tales from the Cumberland Gap*, Detroit: Folklore Associates, 1969. Collected by Gerald Syme in August 1956 from the narration of Rachel Williams of Artemus, Knox County, Kentucky, then aged seventy.

This tale is a particularly artful blend of the standard Cinderella story (AT510a) with incidents from two other widely distributed tales. 'The Spinning-Women by the Spring' (AT480) and 'The Black and the White Bride' (AT403).

'The Spinning-Women by the Spring' is best known as the Grimms' 'Frau Holle' and the British 'Three Heads in the Well'. Its motif of the 'kind and unkind girls' also appears in 'The Black and the White Bride' where it leads up to the animal-transformation of the heroine and bride-substitution, as here and in 'Fair, Brown, and Trembling'.

The story of 'The Three Heads in the Well' features in George Peele's *Old Wives Tale* of 1595, in the chapbook *History of the Four Kings*, and in John Clare's memories in *The Shepherd's Calendar*:

> *The magic fountain where the head*
> *Rose up just as the startld maid*
> *Was stooping from the weedy brink*
> *To dip her pitcher in to drink*
> *That did its half hid mystery tell*
> *To smooth its hair and use it well*
> *Who doing as it bade her do*
> *Turnd to a king and lover too.*

The words spoken by the heads in Rachel Williams's Kentucky version have a long ancestry in England and Scotland.

144

'Rushycoat and the King's Son' is one of many Cinderellas recorded in the United States in this century. These derive from all sorts of traditions (for instance 'An Armenian Cinderella' on p. 46); many, like 'Rushycoat', have close affinities with British tales. Others may be found in Roberts's *South from Hell-for-Sartin*, Richard Chase's *The Jack Tales*, Marie Campbell's *Tales from the Cloud-Walking Country* and other regional collections.

ONCE THERE WAS an old woman had a daughter and she was the ugliest girl in the world. Rushycoat was her stepdaughter and she was the purtiest girl in the world but she had to do all the work and let the others talk and put on. They was a big dance coming up and the woman and her daughter was getting ready to go to it. Rushycoat asked her stepmother to let her go. But no, 'You are a pretty looking thing to go.' And she put a pint of rice in a peck of ashes and told Rushycoat, 'Have all that rice picked out of the ashes and dinner on the table in order when we come back.'

After her and her daughter left Rushycoat commenced picking at the ashes and then her mother appeared to her, dressed her up in the finest clothes and told her to go on to the party. Said she would have the rice picked out of the ashes and the dinner in order on the table when she come back and for her to be back at eleven o'clock. When she got there the King's Son was there and he was the purtiest man in the world. He danced with Rushycoat. She was so purty everybody in the house was looking at her. Even her stepmother and stepsister watched her and didn't know her, she was so purty. And when it was eleven o'clock she quit dancing and went home.

She was back in her old raggedy clothes again and she found the rice out of the ashes and the dinner in order on the table. Her stepmother and stepsister come in just a-talking and carrying on, 'Oh, wouldn't she something now, and dancing with the King's Son.' And the daughter said, 'He might a-got struck on her.' And the woman said, 'You better dance all you can with him tomorrer and not let her beat your time.'

Next day they got ready to go and Rushycoat asked them to let her go and her stepmother said, 'No, now no, you can't go.' She poured another pint of rice in the ashes and told her to have it picked out and the dinner in order when they got back. And so they went on. Soon as they left her mother appeared to her again, give her very fine clothes and some golden slippers and told her to go on and she would have the rice picked out and the dinner on the table when she come at eleven o'clock. She went on again and they still didn't know her. She danced with the King's Son again, almost every dance till eleven o'clock. She waited just about too late. She hurried to get back in time and lost one of her golden slippers.

The King's Son found it. He went around to everybody next day to see who the shoe fit. He said ever who the shoe fit she would be his wife. He come to the ugly girl's house to see if the slipper would fit any of them. The ugly girl cut off her toes and heels trying to get the slipper on. It didn't fit so good and he went on and said he would be back.

They was so afraid he'd find Rushycoat they begin to look for a way to get shet of her. And the stepmother said, 'I'll send her to the end of the world to get a bottle of water.' She baked her up some old skins and some old burned breadcrusts and started her out. She went till dinner and set down to eat. Here come an old man along with a stick in his hand. He said, 'Howdy-do, my granddaughter.'

She said, 'Howdy-do, grandpa.' She said, 'Come and eat some dinner with me.' He set down and eat with her.

When they was through with their crusts, he give her that stick and told her she was going to meet a gang of horses. They would come at her and try to kill her. He said, 'You peck this stick again' the ground and they will walk off.'

She went on till up in the evening and here come a big gang of horses right at her like they was going to run over her. She pecked that stick again' the ground and they just surrounded her and went on. When her supper time come she set down on a bank of the road to eat and here come that old man again. He said, 'Howdy-do, my grand-daughter.'

She said, 'Howdy-do, grandpa.' Said, 'Come and eat with me.'

So they eat. He told her she was going to run into a gang of wild hogs and they would try to eat her up. But she was to keep that stick and peck on the ground and they would not bother her.

She went on along the road till it was getting up about dusty dark and here come a gang of wild shoats and old hogs with tushes a foot long like they was going to tear her up. She pecked the stick again' the ground and they just separated and went on. Rushycoat slept 'side the road and got up early and fixed to eat breakfast. Here come the old man again. They set down and eat. He told her she was going to meet a gang of wild bears and to use the stick like he told her to. The wild bears come at her and she pecked the stick on the ground and they went the other way. At dinner time the old man come again and after eating a bite with her he told her she was nearing the end of the world. She was going to come to a gate and he said, 'When you come to it you peck the stick on the ground and say, "Open, gate, open wide for this fair young lady to go through." ' He said, 'It will open just a little piece and then say again, "Open gate, open wide for this fair young lady to go through to get her a bottle of water." '

She said she would, thanked the man and went on. When she come to the gate she done what the old man had said and after the second time the gate opened and she went on in.

She got to the waterwell and started to put her bottle down, up jumped three bloodyheads and said, 'Wash me and dry me and lay me down easy.'

She washed them and dried them and laid them down easy. She got her water and started on back. The biggest bloodyhead said, 'What do you wish on that fair lady as she goes back home?'

Another un said, 'I wish she smells so good every winder and door on the way will open to her.'

The least one said, 'What do you wish on that fair lady as she goes back home?'

The other said, 'I wish she will be ten times purtier going back as she was coming.'

One said to the last one, 'What do you wish on her?'

He said, 'I wish ever' time she combs her head she will comb a peck of gold off one side and a peck of silver off the other.'

The animals and the people were good to her on the way back. And when she got home she said to her stepmother, 'Comb my head.'

She said, 'Get away from here, I'm not going to comb your lousy head.'

She said, 'I'll comb it myself then.' She begin to comb her head and the gold and silver begin to pour off in her lap. Her stepmother said, 'Come along, my daughter, I'll comb your head.'

She said, 'No, I'll comb it myself,' and she didn't stop till she had combed off a peck of gold and a peck of silver.

The mother told her daughter she was going to send her to the end of the world to get her another bottle of water. She baked her up some fine bread and cakes and started her out. When it come dinner time she set down to eat. Along come an old man with a stick. He said, 'Howdy-do, granddaughter.'

She said, 'You're not my grandpa,' and didn't offer him a bite to eat and he went away. She went on and met up with a gang of wild horses and they just about trampled her to death. Went on till supper time and set down to eat. The old man come up and spoke, 'Howdy-do, grand-daughter.'

She said, 'You're not my grandpa.' He went away and she went on till she met the wild hogs and they like to scared her to death and finally she come to the gate. It opened a little bit for her and she started in and it come back on her and like to pinched her in two. She got on in and come to the well and started to draw up a bottle of water. Up jumped the three bloodyheads and said, 'Wash me and dry me and lay me down easy.'

She said, 'Get away from here, I'm not going to wash you old bloody-heads.'

She started back and the biggest one said, 'Now what do you wish on this foul lady when she gets back home?'

He said, 'I wish she will stink so bad all the winders and doors will be closed to her as she goes back.'

The other one wished that she would be ten times uglier when she got back, and the last one wished when she combed her head she would comb a peck of fleas off one side and a peck of lice off the other. She got back home all right and here come her mother and said, 'Come along, my daughter, and let me comb your hair.'

When she went to combing it the fleas and lice begin to pour in her lap and got all over them.

The King's Son come with the golden slipper and the ugly woman and her daughter got the lice off and hid Rushycoat. The ugly girl put the slippers on without any toes nor heels. They went out and the ugly girl got on a horse 'side King's Son and they started riding down to the church. Riding along and they's a little bird flew up in front of the King's Son's face. It said,

> *Pretty foot, speckled foot, behind the cottage hide,*
> *Ugly foot, speckled foot behind the King's Son ride.*

He said, 'Listen, what is that little bird saying?'

She said, 'You needn't pay any attention to its lies.'
It said it again.

Pretty foot, speckled foot, behind the cottage hide,
Ugly foot, speckled foot behind the King's Son ride.

He said, 'I'm going to see if it's telling a lie.'

He went in behind the henhouse and found Rushycoat. He brought her out and jerked the slippers off the ugly girl and put them on Rushycoat. They just fit her and she was back in her nice clothes again. He helped her up behind him and they went on to the church and got married. The ugly girl and her mother rode along behind them coming back and they stopped to stay all night at a place. Her mother was a witch and so they planned to get shet of her. Her mother witched a pin and had the ugly girl put it in Rushycoat's dress to stick her the next morning.

When they got up to go on the next morning, Rushycoat put on her dress and the pin stuck in her and she turned into a little rabbit and went hopping off into the fields. The King's Son worried and took on over her for a year. But the people shamed him for taking on over a rabbit. So he begin to come and see the ugly girl and took her back to the church and married her, but he was sad over the loss of purty Rushycoat.

They was one of his old men went into the woods to hunt one day and he found a little rabbit hutch. He went in it and there was a little warm bed and in the bed was a little young baby. The other side of the house was just full of gold and silver. He laid down on the other side of the gold and watched what come to tend to that little baby. In come a rabbit and in a minute it had taken off its rabbit hide. And there stood Rushycoat. She went back to the baby and let it nuss and said to it, 'Hush, little King's Son; hush, little King's Son.' She soon went to sleep.

The old man went to the house and called the King's Son out. The ugly wife didn't want him to go out, said the old man was just wanting to tell him a bunch of lies. He went out to him anyway. The old man told him where Rushycoat was at. He gathered him two or three more men and went back to the field where the hutch was. She was gone again. They hid to watch for her to come in. A rabbit come in and took off its fur and there stood Rushycoat. She went and laid down by the baby and called it King's Son. Soon she went to sleep. They slipped up and helt her while the King's Son took up the hide and burnt it. That broke the spell over Rushycoat. The King's Son took her and the baby back home. He run the ugly girl off and him and Rushycoat lived happy ever after.

Cinderella in Tuscany

Source: Alessandro Falassi, *Folklore by the Fireside: Text and Context of the Tuscan Veglia*, Austin, University of Texas Press, 1980.

This account of an evening's tale-telling in which three separate and competing versions of Cinderella are narrated is taken from the chapter entitled 'Fairy Tales for the Young and the Old' in Alessandro Falassi's rich study of the traditional Tuscan evening, the *veglia*. This chapter also contains a splendid version of 'Donkey-Skin'.

Falassi provides photographs of his informants, and a great deal of contextual and analytical information about the material he collected, mainly in 1973 and 1974. His commentary illustrates contemporary folklorists' concern with performance and style and also the application of structuralist ideas to the folktale.

Falassi shows how stories actually get told, which is not always as continuous uninterrupted narratives, but often as John Clare describes in Northamptonshire, 'by starts and fits'.

Let Falassi set the scene:

The children had been murmuring since dinner was over, 'Come on, grandma, tell us a story,' and they kept it up while the table was being cleared and as the dishes were being washed. The old woman procrastinated, and in so doing caused the expectation to grow. She scoffed and joked, being careful, however, not to imply a flat refusal. She made them understand from the tone of her voice and from her replies that she would give in, perhaps: actually, she wanted to be begged, so as to obtain from all who stayed awake an explicit and formal invitation, and an implicit commitment to pay attention and to keep silent. 'No, now there is work to be done . . .' 'But, sweetie, I am dead tired . . .' 'Who can remember stories! Ah, if I could only remember them!'

THAT EVENING an animated discussion began on the variations of Cinderella: some called it the story of Lina, some knew it as Cinderella, others as the Cenderacchiola; Gino repeated: 'No! No! It's the one about the count!'

GRANDFATHER SESTILIO CIONI: Gino knows it, too.

GINO ANICHINI (*friend of grandfather*): No, I heard it was being told to my little girl.

GRANDMOTHER ANNINA: There was a woman who had two children, no . . .

GINO: Three!

GRANDMOTHER: Two! Not three!

GINO: Three! She had two daughters of her own and another one. Whom they kept as . . . They made her into a cinder girl; she sat near the ashes and tended the ashes . . .

GRANDMOTHER: Yes, in short, one of them always remained behind to take care of the ashes and the others went dancing. You're right. So there were three. Well, two or three.

ALESSANDRO FALASSI: But two of them were hers?

GRANDMOTHER: One was not hers and two were hers. So this poor little Cinderella . . . One of them was called . . .

FABRIZIO CIONI (*the seven-year-old*): No, listen, I'll tell it!

GRANDMOTHER: Well, then you tell it.

FABRIZIO: There is . . . there was a man and wife. They got married and they already had two little girls. One day his wife died. So he was left all alone. And he had these two little girls.

GRANDFATHER: Not so loud!

FABRIZIO: One day he went to look for a . . . for a . . . for another woman. And he found one. But this woman . . .

GRANDFATHER: Don't yell!

FABRIZIO: No . . . yes, yes, yes, she had . . .

GRANDMOTHER: Keep quiet, you're getting everything all mixed up.

FABRIZIO: I'm all confused.

GRANDMOTHER: Shut up now, this is how it goes!

FABRIZIO: The man had one daughter and the other woman had two. The stepsisters!

GRANDMOTHER: I'll tell it this way, because there are one hundred ways of telling it. I'll tell it as I remember it. And then . . .

AF: That's right, you tell it as you know it, [to Fabrizio] and then we'll hear the way you know it.

GRANDMOTHER: Yes. I know it this way. There once was a woman and a man and they had two daughters. One always took care of the ashes and the other always went dancing. So . . .

GINO: No, that's a different one!

GRANDMOTHER: In the evening she got all dressed up. You can see that it's another one.

AF: Let's hear yours!

GRANDMOTHER: And she said, 'Well, are you going to the dance tonight?' 'No, no,' she replied. 'I'm not going to the dance because I like to tend the ashes . . .' 'Oh, come on to the dance, you'll see how much fun it is.' 'Hmm. No, no, I'm not coming.' So one day her mother said to her, 'Listen, you have to come to the dance, because if you don't, I'm not going to take your sister either.' But she still refused. At this point, let's see, how does it go . . .

FABRIZIO: Well, it isn't the one that I was thinking of . . .

GRANDMOTHER: Yes, yes, this is how it goes. All right now, all right. So in the evening she had this little bird called Verzicolò, and after the others had gone she said:

> *Verzicolò, little bird,*
> *Make me more beautiful*
> *Than has ever been heard.*

The little bird turned her into a beautiful woman and then she entered the ballroom to dance. But as suddenly as she arrived, just as suddenly she disappeared at midnight. Every evening they saw this beautiful girl enter the ballroom but at a certain moment she would disappear. A young man said, 'Oh, dammit, you'll see; some evening I'm going to get her.'

One evening after the dancing and dancing and dancing, this Cinderella lost a shoe. Oh, dear! The next morning her sister said to her: 'So you didn't come to the dance! But at midnight a beautiful girl came . . . if you would only have seen her . . .' 'Oh, what do I care,' she said. 'I take care of the ashes . . .' 'Oh, come on, always here taking care of the ashes . . .' So this night then she came home missing a shoe, and she said, 'Oh, what should I do, what shall I do, what shall I do.' Then she said, '. . . ah, this young man had the shoe in his pocket; you'll see, she'll come back.' So that evening she ran out after the other had gone to the dance; she started out once more. She started out, however, this time without one shoe. She didn't have the shoe and the little bird was unable to provide her with another one; it did not help her.

> *Verzicolò, little bird,*
> *Make me more beautiful*
> *Than has ever been heard.*

Well, to make it short . . . this young man put the shoe by the door saying, 'I want to see who you are.' When she entered and . . . turned around and saw the shoe at the door, she put it on and danced all night long. He said, 'Now, when you leave, I'll follow you,' this young man said to her. So then while they were dancing her mother recognized her. She stopped her, saying, 'Well, look at you, you must be my daughter.' So when it was time to leave she said to the other sister, call her: 'Lina!' She said. 'Call her, you'll see that that is Lina.' So when they left they both left together.

When they arrived home her mother said to her, 'You came to the dance without saying anything! Ah, but you'll see,' she said. She said to her other daughter: 'I'll show her. You know what we'll make her do tomorrow morning? Tomorrow morning we'll send her to where the kittens live. You'll see that the kittens will scratch her. Tomorrow morning you know what we'll make? We'll make *polenta* [corn bread].' So her mother said to Cinderella, 'You go and get the sieve where the kittens live.' She replied, 'No, I won't go.' 'What do you mean, you won't go; you will go!' Then she said, 'Well, if she won't go then you go.' She told the ugly daughter: 'Listen to me. When you climb the stairs ask if you might have the sieve to make *polenta*. And go slowly because the stairs are made of glass.' And she said nothing to the beautiful daughter. But the beautiful daughter was also intelligent. One day she sent the ugly daughter to get the sieve. And she carefully explained to her how to go about getting it.

GINO: Cinderella!

GRANDMOTHER: No, her sister, the other one. She got to the door and knocked. She said, 'My mother sent me to get the sieve to make *polenta.*' 'Yes, but be careful, the stairs are made of glass.' And she stomped so hard she broke every step. And they gave her the sieve.

When she got back home she said, 'Mamma, I brought you the sieve.' 'Were you careful?' She answered, 'I broke all the steps, and the kittens scratched me all over.' 'Poor thing,' said her mother. 'Now tomorrow morning I'll send Cinderella.' She was well mannered and said to her, 'Go to where the kittens live and take the sieve back.' And so she went slowly, slowly with much care, and didn't break a single step, asking permission of the kittens and the kittens didn't touch her. She gave back the sieve and returned home. Her mother saw that nothing happened to her; how is that possible? 'Tomorrow morning you go back to the kittens again.' 'No, I will not go back there.' She said to the ugly daughter: 'You've got to go back. And along the road when the rooster crows turn around, and when the ass sings don't turn around.' So the ugly daughter took her leave. The rooster crowed and she did not turn around. The ass sang and she turned around, and she grew a long tail. So the next evening . . . the next evening she sent Cinderella saying, 'When the rooster crows, don't turn around, when the ass sings, turn around.' But, instead, when the ass sang she did not turn around. When the rooster crowed she turned around. And a star appeared in the middle of her forehead. So one of them ended up with a star and the other with a tail. But it was beautiful. But this must be only a part of the story.

Annina admitted that her story was perhaps 'not exact'. And Gino replied immediately, 'But you had almost begun the one about . . .' Then she asked him, 'But how does yours go?' And he replied, 'I've always heard my Nunzia tell it this way.' And after a pause he cleared his throat and began:

GINO: The one about the count goes like this. Once there was a woman who had three daughters. She was fond of two of them and could not stand the other one. The third girl always sat near the cinders. One evening the two daughters decided to go to the ball. They told the third daughter they were going to the ball and that she had to stay home and tend the cinders. 'I don't care, I don't care if I stay home,' she replied. 'I don't care, not at all!' So the others went to the ball, and as soon as they arrived at the ball, the fairy appeared to the third sister and turned her into a beautiful woman with beautiful clothes and everything. As they entered the ballroom no one recognized them. Dressed in that way no one knew who she was.

AF: Do you mean the fairy?

GINO: No, the fairy was with her. The one who was with her was the fairy.

FABRIZIO: The fairy was with her.

GINO: So they entered the ballroom and began to dance. 'However,' said the fairy, 'when you dance with someone who asks who you are . . . "I don't know" you have to say, "I don't know!" At midnight on the dot . . .'

FABRIZIO: You have to go home. Leave immediately, eh! Uh, huh!

ROSANNA BERNINI (*age six*): Uh, huh.

GINO: You leave, eh! Me too. Get into the coach and leave. Eh. So she arrived at the ball. There was a count who grabbed this lovely girl and danced with her. 'Miss,' he said, 'tell me, how old are you?' She replied, 'I don't know.' 'Well, where are you from?' 'I don't know.' [The children laugh.]

GRANDMOTHER: He wasn't able to get anything out of her.

GINO: At midnight she was dancing with the count, with this young man. All of a sudden she disappeared. *Boh.* They did not see a thing.

FABRIZIO: Hah, hah.

GINO: This is strange. And she left. And returned home. The other two returned from the dance. They came back from the ball. Cinderella was already back tending the ashes. She was at home again. They said to her: 'If only you could have seen the girl who danced with a young man . . . she was dressed so well . . . she was beautiful! But really beautiful! I've never seen anything like this.'

FABRIZIO: Her sisters! It's that one, it's that one!

GINO: Yes, yes! Well! What do I care . . . what do I care. The next evening the same old thing. The next evening the same thing all over again. They go again to the ball. 'You come along, too,' they said, 'so you can see that girl too, that beautiful girl, she's really something. Oh, come, come, come.' 'No, no, no. I'll not come. I'll stay here; I want to stay here.' And so she stayed home . . . And after the sisters had gone, when they'd already arrived at the ball . . .

FABRIZIO: The fairy appeared again! The fairy came back. She dressed her up!

ROSANNA: Good! Good! And she went to the ball!

GINO: And . . . she began to dance again with the count. Virgin Mary! She was, she was, she was an eyeful for the count! And so during the evening . . . the usual words. 'Miss, where are you from, you didn't want to tell me.' 'I don't know!' [Laughter.]

GRANDMOTHER: God screwed, then!

GINO: 'I don't know!' And everytime he asked her something she replied, 'I don't know.' [Children's laughter.] At midnight the same thing happened again.

FABRIZIO: On the road . . .

ROSANNA: . . . the road.

GINO: Along the road when she was climbing into the coach, she lost a shoe.

ROSANNA: The shoe . . .

GINO: And this count ran and found this shoe. No – Yes! He found this shoe and asked all the women who were at the ball if any of them had lost a shoe. One replied, 'Not I'; another said, 'No'; another said, 'No.' 'Try it on and see who it fits. It doesn't fit anyone.'

ROSANNA: No one!

FABRIZIO: Yes, yes, it's that one, it's that one!

GRANDMOTHER: The one you know, eh!

ROSANNA: It's that one [story]!

GINO: Eh . . . and so there . . . So then what did he do. He went . . . he went down . . . to that family, the one that knew something about the mystery of who the shoe would fit and who it wouldn't fit. He went down there saying, 'But you, housewife, housemother,' however he called her, 'you have three daughters.' She said: 'Yes! I have three. Two are here but the other is always tending the ashes; she's there.' 'Try on this shoe,' he said to the two daughters. 'Does it fit?' 'No.' To the other daughter he said, 'Oh, try it on.' 'No.' 'I'd be pleased if the daughter who takes care of the ashes would try it on too,' said the count.

FABRIZIO: Just in case she would fulfil his eye! He put the shoe on her, and it fit.

GINO: It fit her, he said whoever the shoe fit . . .

FABRIZIO: Will be my wife!

ROSANNA: I'll marry her, I'll marry her!

GINO: And in fact he married her, she became the wife of a count and . . .

FABRIZIO: Rich.

GRANDMOTHER: *And they married and had fun,*
And of this to me they gave none.
They gave me a tiny doughnut.
In that little hole I put it,
And now it's all gone.

[Laughter]

AF: Listen here, didn't that fairy dance?
GINO: No, no, she disappeared.
GRANDMOTHER: Eh, the fairy disappeared.
GINO: She disappeared. She reappeared at midnight.
ROSANNA: Yes.
FABRIZIO: To take her back home.
GINO: To take her away. The . . . fairy accompanied her.

It was at the end of the version proposed by Gino that Fabrizio – at seven years one of the youngest storytellers I have ever listened to – got the attention of the audience after having repeated over and over, 'Can I tell it my way, can I tell it my way?' Finally his grandfather, recognized by his guests as host in charge of the storytelling session, gave his consent. The boy began from the beginning and narrated his version of Cinderella, which previously he had left hanging because he couldn't remember it.

FABRIZIO: Once upon a time there was a man and a woman who got married. The woman . . . they had one daughter. Cinderella. It's almost the same one as he told. It's almost the same. They had one daughter, this man and this woman. The woman died. So he was left alone with his little girl. What did he do? He took another wife. And this one had two daughters. Those two stepsisters that he mentioned.
GINO: So there were three.
FABRIZIO: There were three. They come to three. And this . . . his wife was fond of her two girls, and her husband was fond of his own girl. However, he . . . the two of them were two and the others were three. What could he do? He went to work, and the others made his

157

little girl clean the ashes out of the fireplace because they didn't like her. The others went out dancing. One day something happened, like you said. The fairy appeared. She made Cinderella beautiful. She called for a coach and sent her to the dance. Yes. And she sent her to the dance. Then . . . however, the fairy said, 'At midnight on the dot you must come home because if not next time I won't make you beautiful and I won't let you go to the dance.' When it was midnight 'ding, dong!' The girl, when she heard the clock strike midnight, she ran! Waiting for her . . . waiting for her was the coachman with the carriage. She climbed in and away they went. And she went back among the cinders.

That night when . . . in the morning when she saw her stepsisters, they said to her: 'Virgin Mary, there was a beautiful woman at the dance,' like Gino said . . . 'I would like to know who she was.' [His grandmother laughs.] 'Well,' said Cinderella, 'it certainly wasn't me. Because you always leave me here in the midst of all these ashes.' And . . . 'Well, then, you come this evening,' said her stepsisters. 'No, no, I want to stay here in the cinders with my little cat; it's fun, I play with it, I pet it, I cry . . .' and so on. The following evening, after they had left, the fairy reappeared; she made Cinderella beautiful once more and away she went. Virgin Mary!

GINO: It's very similar, eh!

FABRIZIO: And she kept on dancing with this . . . no like you said in your story, it wasn't a count. It was a . . . king, the son of a king.

GRANDMOTHER: A king!

AF: The son of a king?

FABRIZIO: The son of a king. And so she said to him . . . and so he says: 'Virgin Mary, but that girl there is a real beauty! I must see why it is that she disappears like that at midnight.' And so he puts glue on the stairs. So naturally that evening when midnight came she left the dance, and naturally when she got to the last step where he had put the glue her shoe got stuck. And away she went. She didn't even stop to pick it up. She climbed into the coach and away she went. And she did the same as before. In the evening . . . the next evening the prince didn't see anyone. 'Virgin Mary! Oh, what has she done?' And he found this shoe, the night she ran home. And he said, 'Oh, whose shoe is this?' He tried it on everyone but it fit no one [he hits his fist on the table]. So then he sent . . . what's his name, he sent these . . .

GRANDMOTHER: The coachmen?

FABRIZIO: Not the coachmen. These . . . what did they call those men who went around with megaphones making public announcements . . .

AF: The town crier?

FABRIZIO: Town criers! He sent town criers around. And so they also went to this family and said: 'There's a shoe . . . last evening it was lost! It was lost while she was dancing – whose is it, whose is it?' Everyone came to the door. And the town crier said to the mother, 'It couldn't be yours, could it?' She tried it on; it didn't fit. She said to him: 'I have two daughters. I can let them try it on. I have three. However, I'm not very fond of one of them. You can try it on them.' 'Yes, yes,' he said . . . said the king's son. 'However, I must marry whoever this shoe fits. Even if she's ugly I have to marry her.' And so all three tried the shoe on, but it didn't fit.

GRANDFATHER: Eh, eh, eh!

FABRIZIO: Said the mother: 'I also have this other daughter, another girl who is more pea-brained . . . as we say in Italian, she's always sitting in the cinders . . . she's all . . . she's all covered with ashes . . .'

GRANDMOTHER: Yes, yes, but . . . all this bungling, wait till you hear what comes next. Go on, go on!

GRANDFATHER: Shut up!

FABRIZIO: She's all covered with soot. And you keep quiet! She's all covered with soot. She's all dirty. And so . . . [to his grandmother] you get me all mixed up!

GINO: Go on, go on!

FABRIZIO: And so he said, 'Yes, yes, let's try it on her, too.' When she tried the shoe on, it fit. 'Eh,' said the prince, 'so then this is the shoe that fits . . . that fits that girl who came. Oh, how did someone who's so dirty . . . someone who's so dirty get so beautiful?' [He hits his fist on the table.] The prince sat with his mouth open and said, 'I'll marry her.' And so they left in the town crier's coach and . . . and went to the castle. And the king's son said to the king, 'Father, I have found my bride.' Then the king said, 'Well, when will the wedding take place?' 'On such and such a day,' he said . . . he said. And on such and such a day they got married. And the stepsisters all . . . all . . . all . . . not all . . .

GINO: Dirty?

GRANDMOTHER: Scared!

FABRIZIO: They were . . . not scared. They were . . . [he says excitedly] they wanted to be more beautiful than she was and so they put on some make-up, but they put on so much . . . they seemed to be wearing masks! [Everyone laughs. He continues in an excited tone.] And so then they were so ugly. They got married . . . [slowly, in a lower tone] and . . . they went to the king and lived in the castle happily ever after.

GRANDMOTHER: My goodness, that boy! [She smiles, satisfied.]

That's how Fabrizio got to 'tell it his way.'

The Travellers' Cinderella

Source: From taped recording S A 1976/221/A-B1 in the School of Scottish Studies Sound Archives. Transcribed by Linda Williamson. Narrated by Duncan Williamson to his granddaughters and a niece on 23 November 1976 in a camp on Tarvit Farm, Cupar, Fife.

Duncan Williamson was born in 1928. His second wife, Linda, is currently recording and editing for publication his vast fund of stories. He is deeply committed to the stories he tells and the traveller culture of which they are a part. Such stories are, he suggests, 'telling us how to live in this world as natural human beings'.

This text is unusual among his recorded repertoire for its thick traveller's cant, of which the Williamsons have kindly prepared a glossary (pp. 173–4).

Duncan Williamson's repertoire includes at least four further Cinderella variants. 'Mary Rashiecoats', 'I Love You More than Salt', 'Ashiepet' and one on the 'unnatural father' incest theme. His own comments on 'The Travellers' Cinderella' can be found at the end of the story.

THIS IS THE TRAVELLER version o Cinderella, the way the travellers tell it and how it happened to them ... I mean, things that happens in fairy stories tae other folk happens tae travellers forbyes, ye know!

*

Mary's faither and mother was real travellers an they wannered the country; they had bings o wee weans, all wee steps and stairs. And their auld granny stayed wi them, see? But when Mary was born there was another ten or twelve wee weans on the go, so auld granny bein staying beside them she said tae her dochter Mary's mother, 'You've too many wee weans, an seein I bide mysel, I'm on'y campit aside yese, A'll take the youngest yin and rear her up jist like my ain – it'll gie ye a wee help.'

So her dochter she cried Mary after hersel and the auld granny. The auld woman reared Mary up to a good young woman. And the auld granny used tae wander the roads, read fortunes an sell scrubbers an baskets wherever she could, you see, but Mary was never far awa fae her. She was the bonniest wee lassie ye ever seen.

They wandered here and there and in wintertime they used tae always come tae this big estate, they used tae get campin fae the auld laird. This winter they cam back tae this same campin place – where they stayed was at a crossroads. And up by the crossroads was the big bene cane, where all the bene hantle used tae bing.

But it was late at night when they cam, and the woman says tae the man, 'We'll hev tae get settlit doon fir the wintertime.'

'Oh aye,' he said, 'we'll go back tae where we usually be. The auld laird he's up in years, he disna bother us an we can stay there as long as we like. It's fine and close tae the toon fir aul granny tae wanner inta the hooses.'

But onyway, they pitched their camp fir the wintertime: the man pit up his camp fir tae haud his family an the aul granny pit her ain wee camp a guid wee bit fae the rest o them, and Mary stayed wi her in her camp. But it was aboot, just afore Christmas, when they're sittin aroond their campfire an they seen all this coaches passin.

'The name o God,' says the man, 'whar is all that coaches an horses gaun tae? I never seen so many bonnie horses in ma life and so many bene hantle! I'm gaun up the morn tae play them wi my pipes tae the bene cane.'

The woman says, 'Look, dinna bing up about the bene cane, ye'll get us shiftit. That's all bene hantle gaun up there – the laird's son is comin on twenty-one years the morn. They're havin a great big birthday party fir him. And if you go up there wi your pipes, as low as my faither, ye'll get us shiftit!'

Granny says, 'A'm gaun up the morn among them aa tae read hands.'

'No,' says the woman, 'A'm tellin you, lea the bene hantle alane. You ken the aul laird disna bother hus as long as we stay here . . . don't pay attention tae them.'

But anyway, hit was aboot three o'clock in the afternoon. The auld woman made a drop tea fir her and Mary. Her and Mary made their ain meat, ye see. Mary was aboot eighteen years of age an the bonniest wee lassie ye ever seen in yir life.

She said, 'Granny!'

'What, dochter,' she said, 'what is hit?'

She said, 'Can you tell me somethin?'

'Well,' she said, 'I'll tell ye – I learned ye an awful lot, an if the're onything else ye want tae ken, I'm as well tae tell ye noo.'

She says, 'Granny, whar is all these bonnie bene hantle gaun tae that passes by there?'

She says, 'The young bene cowl up in the big bene cane is havin a party, an he invitit all the young maidens and guries roon aa the country tae come tae his twenty-one o comin of age party. And he's gaunna pick hisself a wife.'

'Oh, Granny-dear,' she said, 'I couldna dae gaun up there!'

'Lassie,' she said, 'what wad you dae up there?'

'Well, I'm a young lassie tae,' she said.

She said, 'Ye ken they dinna take travellers up wi the grand bene canes. Never, Mary, you couldna gang up there.'

'Well, Granny,' she said, 'I could do – A wish A could. If on'y A had the claes an the way o gaun, I wad go in a minute.'

But anyway, wha wannered ower tae the fire tae see Granny but the mother and faither, tae crack tae aul Granny fir a while, ye ken? And the faither heard her.

He said, 'What's this, lassie, this silly notion inta yir heid – you canna go up there among the bene hantle!'

'A wis on'y tellin Granny,' she said, 'I wad like tae go up there an see what's gaun on. Folk must be enjoyin theirsels up there at that big bene cane, an all the lovely claes and all the lovely meat tae eat an everything up there – it must be great. God,' she said, 'I'd been born a young bene mort!'

Granny said, 'Look, I looked after ye tae be –'

'A ken, Granny,' she said, 'ye're good tae me. But I never been in a hoose in ma life an I wad like tae be in, up inta that bene cane among aa these young geds an guries, an gang tae the dance.'

'God bless hus,' said the man, 'that's a funny thing fir a lassie o yir age. Better ye think o a young traveller man tae yirsel, instead o a-speakin aboot a laird's son. You'll never get nae laird's son!'

'You never know,' says aul Granny, 'what she may get yet afore she's aff the worl.'

But anyway, they sut and crack't fir a long while an the man and woman wannered awa tae their own camp, ye see. An Mary's sittin, her heid hangin doon, see. Aul Granny went away back inta the tent her ainsel, an she's mumblin away tae her ainsel at the back o the camp.

Mary said, 'Wha're ye speakin tae at the back –'

'I'm no speakin tae naebody, lassie,' she said. The aul granny cam oot and she had a hankie tied on her head. She had all her fancy earrings on and all her fancy jewellery on, aa hangin aboot her.

'Granny-dear,' she said, 'what are ye dressed up for? Ye're no gaun tae the party, are ye?'

'Oh, no me, Mary,' she said, 'I'm no gaun tae the party. But I'll tell ye . . . dinna tell yir naiscowl or yir naismort, but ye're gaun tae the party!'

'What?' said Mary. 'I cannae!'

'Wait,' she says, 'don't tell them a thing! But I'll tell ye. You wait and you dae what I tell ye, an you'll get tae the party aa right! Listen, remember one thing: the party starts tonight, but at twelve o'clock keep yir ee oot the room window, an when ye see the moon full the night, mak sure – that party'll gang on ti hours in the mornin – but you make sure that you be back afore the moon starts tae drop.'

'But, Granny,' she says, 'I'm no awa yet! Hoo can I – I canna gang tae a party. Look at me, A'm a bundle o rags! The folk wad chase me fir ma life if A went up there like that.'

'Dinna you worry,' says Granny, 'jist you wait!'

Way Granny goes tae a wee pond at the back o the camp, she gets a crooked stick, an auld staff she had, an she cleiks two puddocks oot, ties them in her hankie. She taks them back. And she goes roon the back o the camp where she's cuttin vegetables an she gets a great big monster cabbage leave – she brings that back wi her.

Mary's sittin watchin her. 'Granny, Granny,' she said, 'what're ye gaun tae do wi that?'

'Never mind, lassie,' she said. 'Mary, get on!'

'What is hit?' she said.

She said, 'Dae ye see thon white butterflee? Catch him tae me!' The white butterflee's stottin, stottin, stottin round the camp, ken, in the gloamin, just comin in the evenin. Mary's after it – snap, catcht the white butterflee an brung it back.

'Noo, Mary,' she says, 'whatever you see happenin, never mention it!'

Aul Granny took oot this wee thing like a long stick wi a bunch o stars on it. And she touched this cabbage leaf, an afore you could say a word, it was the bonniest gleamin glass coach you ever seen in yir life! She pulled half a dozen lang hairs oot o her heid and she made harness, put it on the puddocks for harness; and she toucht the two puddocks, she touched the hairs – they turned inta two white horses inta the coach wi lovely silver-mountit harness. And she catcht the butterflee, toucht the butterflee, and there he was dressed – snow-white footman – dressed in white an a big tile hat sittin in front o the carriage. She done the same tae Mary an she turned Mary inta a grand bene mort!

Granny's mumblin away tae hersel; Mary's in the coach now sittin. Who comes over but her faither and mother! Now the coach is lyin across fra the auld woman's camp, and when Mary's faither an mither sees this, she says, 'Shanness, shanness, we're quodit – the bene hantle, the bene hantle must hae went aff the road. That auld wumman's sprachin 'em for looer. Mother, ye're gaunna get us quodit! That's the bene hantle. What di' you stop the bene hantle's coach fir? I warnt you not to be readin hands, the bene hantle's hands!'

The footman he's sittin, 'on white dickie on his neck, white bow on his neck, an he's not sayin a word! An thes two beautiful white horses and this grand young bene mort's lyin back in this coach.

'Right,' says Granny tae the footman, 'drive on!'

Away goes the coach.

'But, Mother,' says the dochter tae the aul granny, 'what were you mangin tae the bene hantle? Are you wantin tae get hus shiftit?'

She says, 'A wasna mangin . . . the coach went aff this road, and I didna ken – they wantit tae ken the road tae the bene cane an I tellt them tae gang straight on.' See, she never said a word!

Anyway, by this time the footman druv Mary's coach up – it was the last tae the castle. In the big square the coaches was sittin in dozens. And the folk was jist about tae go inta the party, when in comes this coach: there never was a coach in the country like it, an there weren't a matcht pair o horses nor silver harness you'd ever seen in the country. And this footman's sittin on the coach – six foot he was and dressed in white. Then he stepped doon, he opened the door and this lassie cam oot. The folk's breath was tooken away when they seen this lassie comin oot – she was just like an angel. Even her very shoes was made of glass on her feet, and they were that tiny. Oh, every folk bowed when they seen her comin, they thought she was some queen or some princess away fae some foreign land, she was the last coach in. And the young laird his ainsel he run oot, met her an invited her inta the great big parlour. And when he took her into this place . . . there were dozens of lords and ladies all sittin round, ye ken, drinkin and carryin on . . . Mary was just like an angel.

Cam in and oh, they made the best for 'em, put her sittin down an gev her everything. The young laird couldna take his een aff her, couldna take his een aff her ataa! And all the guries is trying tae get in close tae her, but na, it was nae use. But he wouldna have nothin tae do wi them. And he danced wi Mary – she was as licht as a butterflee! Aul Granny made the enchantment tae her, made her could dance like a butterflee. And the laird was that happy he didna see the time passin, an he was waltzin round this great big room. And Mary lookit oot, oot through the window, she seen the moon was full as could be right above i' the sky. She excused hersel, and out through the hall door. Jist as she's gaun oot, the first step, she slippit and yin o the shoes fell ahind her; but she never stopped, she kept goin. And by the time she reached the foot o the step she was back to her ainsel – two bare feet, long black hair hangin down her back, ragged dress on her. Gone was the coach, gone was the footman, gone was the lot. And one of the guards standin at the gate looked at her passin by.

The laird's oot and he's down the steps, he seen the shoe lyin and he liftit it. He says tae one o the guards that were at the door, 'Did ye see the beautifulest lady in the world passin by here?'

'No me,' says the guard. 'Laird, there naethin passed here but some o these gypsy brats fra the tinkers' camp doon there. I seen her runnin down that road wi her bare feet.'

'Impossible,' says the laird, 'it's impossible! The're no gypsy brats here; my lady wis here . . . she's gone. Where did she disappear tae, where's her coach, why di' you not stop them, stop the coach till I cam oot?'

'Ma lord,' he said, 'I never saw any coach.'

'Were you asleep, man?' he said. 'Look, the're her shoe, an her glass coach was here an her footman wis here waitin on her. You must have seen them! I'll deal with you in the morning!'

He goes back in, but ach na, his night was finished, his heart was broken. His heart was broken, didna ken what tae dae. All the folk packed up, they seen that it was finished; and he never spoke tae any – oh, hunderds o guries – but he never spoke to a soul. He was sittin and his aul faither cam into him.

'What's wrong wi you, laddie,' he said till him, 'my son, what's wrong wi you?'

'Well, Father, it's like this,' he said, 'the loveliest thing in the world came to me last night at my party and she danced wi me all night. And she mysteriously disappeared out o my life; she has drivin me crazy and I don't know what's wrong wi me. I –'

'Well,' said the father, 'there's on'y one thing for it – tomorra morning – I've got plenty horses and plenty men in the estate – we'll find her again fir ye. Hev ye something that you'll know her by; d'ye know her name?'

'No me, I don't know her name.'

'Why didn't you find her name?'

He says, 'I never asked her name.'

'Where did she come fae? What was her footman like? What kind o coach . . .' he said.

The young laird tellt his faither.

Na, the next day and for three days after that, the young laird sent men all over the country searchin for this coach an this young lady; but na, it was impossible.

Aul Granny she was up the back door o the big hoose and she read all the fortunes, read the cook's hand, and she got stuff at the back door. They were all telling her this story about the lovely maiden that cam to the thing. Aul Granny never said a word, see! Back doon.

Her son-in-law Mary's faither says tae aul granny, 'The tell me the're a wild carry-on up at the big hoose the other night.'

'Aye, there were a wild carry-on,' she says. 'Some kind o carry-on, o some kind o lassie that cam tae the party and the laird's ga'n aff his heid, canna get her. She disappeared.'

'God bless me,' says the man.

So they bade there fir about three days. And there were all riders passin by but they never looked at the travellers' camp.

So one day the laird's sittin, his faither cam tae him, says, 'What's wrong, son?'

'Well, Father, tae tell you the truth,' he says, 'I'm completely heart-broken, I can't go on any longer.'

'What way,' he says, 'you can't go on any longer?'

'Well, I've searched men all over the country,' he says, 'and the coach couldna go oot no farther away in three days as a fast horseman could go. They can't be gotten in the district, she never was sawn, she completely vanished off the face o the earth.'

Faither said, 'I doot, son, the're some enchantment attached tae this.'

'Enchantment, my,' he said, 'Daddy, you know the're no such a thing!'

He said, 'Heve you nothing that you would know her by?'

'Yes, Father,' he said, 'A've got one thing.'

'What is it?'

He said, 'One o her shoes.'

'Well, it's simple tae dae, isn't it? Jist go oot tomorrow,' he said, 'and take some men with you, search the country! And every woman you come tae, try the shoe on her foot; the foot that fits, that'll be – enchantment or no enchantment – that'll be the body.' He said, 'If that shoe wis special made –' the aul man looked at it, made o glass, pure crystal glass – he said, 'it'll not fit another fit but the fit it was meant ta fit.'

'Faither,' he said, 'ye're right. I'll dae that.'

He called all his men tae him the next mornin, pickit five o the best yins, five fast horses. And the young laird's wi them, away they go. And they're round the country, round and round and round the country all fearin day. Na! Tryin everybody; lassies tried tae crush their feet inta it, but na, it was nae use. Some o them tried tae get their toe inta it, and it's killin their feet trying tae get inta this glass shoe. Yinst or twice the laird thocht it was gaunna fit on somebody's fit, then na, never; then he was sick.

But on the road back he cam up the road ga'n tae the castle. He hears the lauchin an gigglin and carryin on, you see; this was the wee weans bleggerin. He stops his horse, says, 'What's that over there?'

'Oh, my lord, that's nothing concernin you.'

He says, 'What do ye mean, "it's nothing concerning me"?'

'Oh,' he said, 'that's a tinkers' encampment.'

'Well,' he said, 'if it's a tinkers' encampment, what difference does it make? They'll hev women and their girls.'

'Oh, ma lord,' he said, 'no, no, no! These girls, these are people – tinker people of the road – travellers, tinkers, gypsies!'

'It makes no difference tae me,' he said, 'if they're gypsies or what they are. If the're young girls in them,' he said, 'how do you know what's there? Come over wi me!'

The bene cowl rode over tae the travellers' camp and his six men wi him. And the aul man mang't tae his woman, 'Oh shanness, shanness, that's hus shiftit noo,' he said, 'that's the quod. A mang't aboot yir naismort bingin up, sprachin aboot the bene cane. A jant, A jant we're gaun tae be shiftit. That was yir mother, yir aul mother up readin fortunes at the back o the bene cane.' He said, 'That's the bene gadgie doon noo ower the heid o it. That's the road fir hus the morn.' Man cam oot, ye ken. 'Well, ma lord, what is hit, what are ye here aboot?'

'Well, to tell ye the truth, ma man,' the bene cowl said, 'I'm not here aboot nothing.'

'We're not doin ye, doin any harm?'

'No, no,' he said, 'we're not here to shift ye or do any harm; we're just makin an inquiry.'

'Oh,' he said, 'ye're makin an inquiry . . . What kin o inquiry?'

'Well,' he said, 'I'll tell ye: three nights ago A gev a party for my twenty-oneth birthday,' and the man explained the story tae him.

The traveller man said, 'Yes –'

'And,' he said, 'the last to arrive was a coach, a crystal coach, an one footman an one young maiden.'

'You're right enough,' says the traveller man, 'you're richt enough. They wis stopped here.'

'What!' says the laird.

He says, 'They were stopped at this very bit!'

'Cah, guid enough,' says the laird, 'at last, at last! I've got some word o them. Did ye talk to them?'

'No me.'

'Oh, at's a pity.'

'Ah, but wait a minute.'

'It's a pity you didna talk tae them or found out something aboot them,' says the laird. Now he begun tae shake wi excitement.

'Ah, but wait a minute,' he says, 'ma wife's aul mother in the next camp here she wis crackin tae them. I mind o her crackin tae the bene mort in the coach, I think she read her hand or tellin fortunes or something.'

Bene cowl says, 'Here, aul lady, come here!'

'What is it?' she said.

He said, 'Come here, my aul lady, don't be afraid, don't be afraid. I'll make it worth your while if you can help me.'

'What is hit,' she said, 'ma lord?'

He tellt her the story. 'Oh aye,' she said, 'the coach. Oh, but I couldna help ye.'

'Well,' he said, 'I've searched the country high and low.'

'Oh,' she said, 'they stopped here an asked me two three questions, an I directed them up tae the castle. That's all A ken aboot them.'

Anyway, he said, 'I'm sorry,' an he pit his hand in his pocket, he plunked the aul woman a gold sovereign. 'That'll help ye,' he said, 'aul Granny.'

'Thank you, sir,' she said.

And just like that, as he begin' tae gang awa, who cam oot but Mary. And the laird lookit, says, 'Who's the girl?'

She says, 'That's ma granddaughter.'

'Is it?' he says. 'Come here, my girl!'

'Shanness, shanness,' says the lassie's mother, 'we're quodit.'

'What ye quodit for?' says the granny.

And this foreman o the head bene cowl says, 'Ma lord, that's a tinker.'

He says, 'I don't care, suppose it's Satan – she's got a foot, doesn't she?'

'Oh yes,' he said, 'and two lovely feet she has got!'

'Well,' he said, 'get the shoe and try it on her foot! She's as good as anybody else.' Bene cowl flung his leg off the horse and down he comes, red ridin breeches on him, says, 'Come here, my young woman!'

Mary wannered ower, ken. Oh, young ged, twenty-one he was. And she's about eighteen, see, bonnie lassie. She had her bare feet, bonnie wee tidy feet she had.

He says, 'Put yir foot on my knee.'

'No me, sir,' she says, 'I'm no puttin ma foot –'

He says, 'Put yir foot on my knee!'

She says, 'What fir? Wh–why should I put ma foot on yir knee?'

He said, 'I want tae try a shoe on yir foot.'

She said, 'I never wear shoes, I go in my bare feet.'

'Well,' he said, 'look, I've been aroond all the country and prob'ly you've heard the story; and if this shoe fits yir foot, you're what I'm lookin fir!'

Now she jant, see, Mary kent. She held her foot oot – slip, on her fit – just fittit neet.

'You're her,' says the laird, 'you're my queen, my princess!'

'Ay,' says the auld woman.

He says, 'That's her.'

She says, 'That's her.'

'Well,' he says, 'she must go –'

'No, no,' says the auld woman. 'No, no, you can't take her.'

'Oh, but,' says the laird, 'I'm takin her. She's mine, A got her.'

'No, no,' she says, 'she's my granddaughter.'

'But,' he says, 'A must have her.'

The man and her mother comes over, 'What's wrong, Granny?' he says.

She says, 'That man wants tae tak the wee lassie awa.'

He says tae the laird, 'What do ye mean – she never done nae harm – was she up at yir castle stealin or something?'

'No, no, no, no,' he says. 'That's the girl!'

'Tha–h–h,' says the auld man, 'that's no the girl, the're some mistake somewhere.'

He says, 'The're no mistake, the're not another foot in the world that that shoe'll fit but one. And she's hit. And I must have her.'

'Well,' says the auld woman, 'if it must be, it must be. I'll take Mary up tae you later on in the day – Mary's her name – I'll deliver her tae ye in the afternoon.'

'Well,' said the laird, 'if ye don't, A'll be back.'

Her father and mother said, 'Look, she's only a tinker, a trav –'

He said, 'It makes no difference tae me what she is – she's mine and I want her.'

'Well,' said her father, 'if you want her, you better be good to her!'

'Oh, I'll be good tae her,' he said, 'don't worry, A'll look after her.' He says tae her, 'Keep the shoe. But remember, tonight the're gaun to be a bigger party an I'll be expectin ye there!'

So the laird rode up tae the castle and sent word, he sent all the men he had right through all the country, telling them, everybody tae come – tonight. The laird had found his princess and he was gaunnae have a bigger party, largest party in the country. He tellt his faither that he had found his princess; he never said whar he got her, ye ken!

When the laird goes away, ower comes Mary's faither and mother tae the aul granny. He says, 'Granny, whit were ye mangin tae the bene cowl? That lassie's no nae princess! You're gaunnae get hus banished, we're gaunnae be quodit. If you send her in that bundle o rags up there at two o'clock tae the big party, we'll be all jailed an the rest o the wee weans will all be tooken off hus. I'm shiftin – I'm bingin avree!'

'No, no,' she says, 'everything's all right.'

'Ay, witch,' he said, 'A ken. I ken, witch, wi you workin yir witch-craft, I ken aa aboot ye. Many's a thing, trouble, you got hus in afore wi your spells an your witchcraft, I ken aa aboot you! But I'm shiftin.'

'No,' she said, 'you're no shiftin. You stay where ye are and every-thing'll be all right. So Mary's gaunnae marry the young laird – 'twill be the best thing that ever happened. Look, your dochter married tae the laird, you can come here an camp all the days o yir life and naebody never bother ye, ye'll be well off for ever.'

He said, 'Ye're gaunna get me banished.'

'No,' she said, 'you'll no be banished. Leave it tae me.'

'All right, witch,' he said, 'we'll leave it to you.' He went away tae his ain camp.

Two o'clock in the day comes again. Back goes aul granny: another two puddocks, another cabbage leaf, half a dozen hairs out o her heid, pulls them oot, harness the two puddocks, maks Mary catch another butterflee, same coach back over again, puts Mary back the same way as she was . . . 'Right, footman, drive on!'

Footman drove away up to the castle; Mary cam out. The young laird ran oot, kissed her and cuddled her, arms round her neck an took her into the parlour. He said, 'Come and meet my daddy.' Took her and showed her tae his faither. He said, 'Father, at last I've found my princess and I'll be happy for evermore. Oh,' he said tae a man, 'by the way, go out tae the door and fetch in the footman, give him something tae drink and get my sweetheart's horses stabled for her at wonst!'

Out he goes, this man goes oot . . . nothing. Two big puddocks away hoppin tae the road and a wee cabbage leaf, it aa withered blowin awa wi the wind – nothing – all was gone. And Mary married the young laird and lived happy ever after and they hev a big family. And the auld traveller man campit there all the days o his life, every winter ti his family was growed up, and that's the last o my wee story!

*

That was the travellers' idea how Cinderella really was for them. My father tellt it tae me years and years ago when we were wee. I heard it the other way, I got it in school and I read about it in a pantomine and I seen it in a picture, but hit was never the same. I thocht it was better – I mean, ye heard it first that way, the way I'm after tellin ye a minute ago – that was Cinderella in wir life. The other way meant nothing tae me because I wasnae in the other life, that was fir the country folk, fir the country folk's way. The travellers had their ain way o it and the country folk had their ain way. I just liked the way I heard it . . . and who knows that wir travellers' way wasna the true way or the first way! It could hae been real, I mean the real Cinderella could be taken aff the travellers' story, couldn't it?

Ay, around Christmas time it was . . . see, they cam back, the auld traveller man and woman and the auld granny cam back tae the estate every year. The aul granny was supposed tae be a witch, ye see, an aul witch.

Glossary of Scots and traveller cant

A – I (unemphatic)
alane – alone
at – that
aul(d) – old
avree – away
ay – yes
bene – good, grand
bing – go; come
bings – plenty
bleggerin – wrestling in fun
camp – tent; encampment
cane – house
claes – clothes
cleiks – hooks, seizes
cowl – man
crack – discuss things
country folk – non-travellers
dinna – don't
drop – small amount of

ee(n) – eye(s)
fae, fra – from
fearin – entire
fit – foot
gadgie – man
gang – go
gaun – going
geds – young men
gloamin – twilight
guries – girls
hantle – people
hit – it (emphatic)
hus – us (emphatic)
jant – knew
kent – knew
lea – leave
looer – money
mangin – speaking, saying
mort – woman

naiscowl – father
naismort – mother
neet – exactly
plunked – pitched
puddocks – frogs
quodit – jailed
shanness – shame (on us)
sprachin – begging
stottin – going zig-zag
the morn – tomorrow
the night – tonight

the're – there is, there was
tidy – nice
tile – tall
till – to
two three – a few
wad – would
wanner – wander
weans – wee ones, children
wonst – once
worl – world
yin – one

Further Reading

AARNE, Antti, *The Types of the Folktale: A Classification and Bibliography*, translated and enlarged by Stith Thompson, 2nd revision, Helsinki, Academia Scientiarum Fennica, 1961 (Folklore Fellows Communications no. 184)

BAUGHMANN, Ernest W., *Type and Motif Index of the Folktales of England and North America*, The Hague, Mouton & Co., 1966 (Indiana University Folklore Series no. 20)

BETTELHEIM, Bruno, *The Uses of Enchantment: The Meaning and Importance of Fairy Tales*, London, Thames & Hudson, 1976; New York, Vintage Books, 1977

BOLTE, Johannes, and Polívka, George, *Anmerkungen zu den Kinder-u. Hausmärchen der Brüder Grimm*, 5 vols., Leipzig, Dieterich'sche Verlagsbuchhandlung, 1913–32

BRIGGS, Katharine, *A Dictionary of British Folk-Tales in the English Language. Incorporating the F. J. Norton Collection*, 4 vols., London, Routledge & Kegan Paul; Bloomington, Indiana University Press, 1970–71

COX, Marian Roalfe, *Cinderella. Three hundred and forty-five variants of Cinderella, Catskin, and Cap O' Rushes, abstracted and tabulated, with a discussion of mediaeval analogues, and notes*, with an introduction by Andrew Lang, London, David Nutt for the Folklore Society, 1893; reprinted Nendeln, Liechtenstein, Kraus Reprint Limited, 1967

DUNDES, Alan, *Cinderella: A Folklore Casebook*, New York & London, Garland Publishing, 1982

ELLIS, John M., *One Fairy Story Too Many: The Brothers Grimm and their Tales*, Chicago & London, University of Chicago Press, 1983

GRIMM, Jacob Ludwig Karl, and Grimm, Wilhelm Karl, *Grimms' Tales for Young and Old*, translated by Ralph Mannheim, New York,

Doubleday & Co., 1977; London, Victor Gollancz, 1978, Penguin Books, Harmondsworth, 1984

PERRAULT, Charles, *Contes*: textes établis, avec introduction, sommaire biographique, bibliographie, notices, relevé de variantes, notes et glossaire par Gilbert Rouger, Paris, Classiques Garnier, 1967

Perrault's Popular Tales, edited from the original editions, with introduction, etc., by Andrew Lang, Oxford, Clarendon Press, 1888

The Fairy Tales of Charles Perrault, translated by Angela Carter, London, Victor Gollancz, 1977

OPIE, Iona, and Opie, Peter, *The Classic Fairy Tales*, London, Oxford University Press, 1974

ROCKWELL, Joan, *Evald Tang Kristensen: A Lifelong Adventure in Folklore*, Aalborg & Copenhagen, Aalborg University Press and the Danish Folklore Society, 1982

ROOTH, Anna Birgitta, *The Cinderella Cycle*, Lund, C. W. K. Gleerup, 1951

THOMPSON, Stith, *The Folktale*, New York, Holt, Rinehart & Winston, 1946, reprinted Berkeley, Los Angeles and London, University of California Press, 1977

Motif-Index of Folk-Literature: A Classification of Narrative Elements in Folktales, Ballads, Myths, Fables, Mediaeval Romances, Exempla, Fabliaux, Jest-Books and Local Legends, revised and enlarged edition, 6 vols., Copenhagen, Rosenkilde & Bagger, 1955–8

TING, Nai-Tung, *The Cinderella Cycle in China and Indo-China*, Helsinki, Academia Scientiarum Fennica, 1974 (Folklore Fellows Communications no. 213)

ZIPES, Jack, *Breaking the Magic Spell: Radical Theories of Folk and Fairy Tales*, London, Heinemann Educational Books, 1979

Acknowledgements

The author and publisher would like to thank the owners of copyright material for their permission to reproduce the following stories:

'Cendrillon', translation copyright © Neil Philip and Nicoletta Simborowski, 1989.

'Yeh-hsien', reprinted by permission of The Folklore Society.

'Kajong and Haloek', translation copyright © Neil Philip and Nicoletta Simborowski, 1989.

'Benizara and Kazekara', reprinted by permission of Chicago University Press from Keigo Seki, *Folktales of Japan*, copyright © 1963 by The University of Chicago. All rights reserved.

'Burenushka, the Little Red Cow', from *Russian Fairy Tales*, collected by Aleksandr Afanas'ev, translated by Norbert Guterman. Copyright © 1945 by Pantheon Books, Inc., and renewed 1973 by Random House, Inc. Reprinted by permission of Pantheon Books, a Division of Random House, Inc.

'The Poor Girl and her Cow', reprinted from *Folk Tales of 'Iraq*, translated by E. S. Stevens (1931), by permission of Oxford University Press.

'An Armenian Cinderella', reprinted by permission of Wayne State University Press from Susie Hoogasian-Villa, *100 Armenian Tales*, copyright © Wayne State University Press, 1966. All rights reserved.

'Askenbasken, who Became Queen', translation copyright Joan Rockwell, 1989.

'Mossycoat', printed by permission of the Estate of T. W. Thompson and The Brotherton Library, Leeds.

'Dona Labismina', translation copyright © Lourdes Gonçalves and Neil Philip, 1989.

FOR THE BEST IN PAPERBACKS, LOOK FOR THE

In every corner of the world, on every subject under the sun, Penguin represents quality and variety – the very best in publishing today.

For complete information about books available from Penguin – including Pelicans, Puffins, Peregrines and Penguin Classics – and how to order them, write to us at the appropriate address below. Please note that for copyright reasons the selection of books varies from country to country.

In the United Kingdom: Please write to *Dept E.P., Penguin Books Ltd, Harmondsworth, Middlesex, UB7 0DA*

If you have any difficulty in obtaining a title, please send your order with the correct money, plus ten per cent for postage and packaging, to *PO Box No 11, West Drayton, Middlesex*

In the United States: Please write to *Dept BA, Penguin, 299 Murray Hill Parkway, East Rutherford, New Jersey 07073*

In Canada: Please write to *Penguin Books Canada Ltd, 2801 John Street, Markham, Ontario L3R 1B4*

In Australia: Please write to the *Marketing Department, Penguin Books Australia Ltd, P.O. Box 257, Ringwood, Victoria 3134*

In New Zealand: Please write to the *Marketing Department, Penguin Books (NZ) Ltd, Private Bag, Takapuna, Auckland 9*

In India: Please write to *Penguin Overseas Ltd, 706 Eros Apartments, 56 Nehru Place, New Delhi, 110019*

In Holland: Please write to *Penguin Books Nederland B.V., Postbus 195, NL–1380AD Weesp, Netherlands*

In Germany: Please write to *Penguin Books Ltd, Friedrichstrasse 10–12, D–6000 Frankfurt Main 1, Federal Republic of Germany*

In Spain: Please write to *Longman Penguin España, Calle San Nicolas 15, E–28013 Madrid, Spain*

In France: Please write to *Penguin Books Ltd, 39 Rue de Montmorency, F–75003, Paris, France*

In Japan: Please write to *Longman Penguin Japan Co Ltd, Yamaguchi Building, 2–12–9 Kanda Jimbocho, Chiyoda-Ku, Tokyo 101, Japan*

A selection from the Penguin Folklore Library

Irish Folktales Edited by Henry Glassie

From the wild western coast to the urban bustle of Belfast and Dublin, from the ancient world of the Druids to the Celtic Renaissance and the present day, here are 125 marvellous Irish tales, told in the great Irish tradition.

Arab Folktales Translated by Inea Bushnaq

'This is a book to be read and re-read many times: its pleasures are of the ages. Rarely has a people's authentic spirit been so close to hand' – Edward W. Said

Italian Folktales Selected and retold by Italo Calvino

'A magic book and a classic' – *Time*

'Calvino possesses the power of seeing into the deepest recesses of human minds and bringing their dreams to life' – Salman Rushdie in the *London Review of Books*

A Thorn in the King's Foot Stories of the Scottish Travelling People
Duncan and Linda Williamson

Duncan Williamson has spent many years on the road, listening, learning and retelling the folklore of his nation. This unique collection is drawn from his vast repertoire – tales from a thriving oral tradition, both simple and sophisticated, sometimes witty, sometimes sad.

Elijah's Violin and other Jewish Folktales Selected and retold by Howard Schwartz

A glorious treasury of Jewish tales from fifth-century Babylon to nineteenth-century Europe.

'I rejoice in the splendour – imagination's bliss – of Howard Schwartz's collection' – Cynthia Ozick